THE CRAFT OF THE
JAPANESE SCULPTOR

THE CRAFT OF THE
JAPANESE SCULPTOR

BY LANGDON WARNER

New York

McFarlane, Warde, McFarlane

and Japan Society of New York

1936

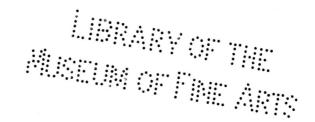

DESIGNED BY FREDERIC WARDE

PRINTED IN THE UNITED STATES OF AMERICA

OKAKURA KAKUZO

in piam memoriam

ACKNOWLEDGMENTS

MY *thanks for permission to use their illustrations are due to:*

Mr. S. Ogawa of Asuka-en Photographers; Nara

Messrs. Yamanaka & Co.; Osaka

The Imperial Museum; Nara

Howard Mansfield Esq.; New York

Museum of Fine Arts; Boston

Nelson Gallery; Kansas City

Professor Muneyoshi Yanagi; Tokyo

Rubel Asiatic Research Bureau, Fogg Museum; Cambridge

I am indebted, also, to the various owners who have given me permission to reproduce their objects.

Contents

Plates

My special gratitude is due to Mr. Ogawa, Director of the Asuka-en Photographic Firm in Nara, who most courteously has given me his consent to reproduce his admirable photographs.

PLATES

NARA PERIOD

16. *Armature for Hollow Lacquer Statue, Akishino Temple, Nara*
17. *Guardian King, Todaiji Temple, Nara*
18. *Detail of Guardian King, Todaiji Temple, Nara*
19. *Detail of Kasenyen, Kofukuji Temple, Nara*
20. *Ashira-O, Kofukuji Temple, Nara*
21. *Detail of Fukukenjaku Kwannon, Todaiji Temple, Nara*
22. *Detail of Mine-no-Yakushi, Horyuji Temple, Nara*
23. *Detail of Guardian King, Akishino Temple, Nara*
24. *Guardian, Todaiji Temple, Nara*
25. *Bon Ten, Todaiji Temple, Nara*
26. *Monju, Horyuji Temple, Nara*
27. *Detail of Buddha, Kanimanji Temple, Nara*
28. *Detail of plate 27*
29. *Gong, Kofukuji Temple, Nara*
30. *Detail of Engraving on Lotus Petal of the Pedestal of the Daibutsu, Todaiji Temple, Nara*
31. *Lantern, Todaiji Temple, Nara*
32. *Detail of plate 31*
33. *Shuho-O Bosatsu, Toshodaiji Temple, Nara*
34. *Detail of Yoryu Kwannon, Daianji Temple, Nara*
35. *Dramatic Mask, Todaiji Temple, Nara*

JOGAN PERIOD

36. *Buddha, Muroji Temple, Nara*
37. *Detail of plate 36*
38. *Unknown Nyorai, Toshodaiji Temple, Nara*

ASHIKAGA PERIOD

MOMOYAMA PERIOD

TOKUGAWA PERIOD

PLATES

THE CRAFT OF THE
JAPANESE SCULPTOR

The things which men have made . . . are inevitably the best witness. They cannot lie, and what they say is of supreme importance. For they speak of man's soul and they show who are his gods.

Sculpture, BY ERIC GILL

Introduction

SINCE this book is not meant for specialists or for students beginning to specialize but for the general public, I have tried to avoid all facts that seem even once removed from the immediate uses of sculpture itself.

Those things that are immediately necessary to know while we are looking at an object made by another man are:

> its purpose,
>
> its materials and manner of making,
>
> its formal image in the maker's mind.

Now the last of these is hard to come by when that mind is another's and he a foreigner long dead. It is therefore necessary to recapture what we can of his particular image through the hints of history, the study of his religion as well as the examination of past fashions and of likes and dislikes current in his time but not with us. It is here we see how to use the secondary facts one or more removed from the essentials we look at.

Only by knowing something of the sculptor's purpose, his manner of making and of the particular ideas that limit or set free his imagination can we appreciate the perfection of what he makes. And only by a sound grasp of the degree of perfection he has arrived at, can we get a proper sense of what beauty may lie in his sculpture. But, and this is of prime importance, we are interested solely in his success in achieving his own ends (not ours) with his own materials (not our choice) on his own plan. Any other basis for judgement or attempted appreciation would manifestly be useless.

To clear our minds of the methods sometimes used by historians of art and to keep them precisely focussed on the essentials is in reality the difficult and scholarly thing to do. For tabulating dates and memorizing them is simple and has nothing in it of the high intellectual task that confronts the scholar.

What then of beauty? Can mere information concerning the essentials in a statue take the place of that quickening of the pulse I know for a sign that I have loved? Obviously it can never take its place. But only a mind informed, in the philosophical sense, can detect true beauty or be sensitive to it.

I must learn the foreign language in which the sonnet is written, I must then comprehend its particular meaning, I must appreciate its lovely joinery and, lastly, I must catch what I can of the formal beauty in the poet's mind—the form he heard in the mind's ear and tried to set down in words.

It is not otherwise with the beauty of sculpture.

The statues illustrated in this small book were made by carvers and modellers after things that were seen in their minds. One look at them is enough to demonstrate that they were not copies made in wood or bronze or clay from natural models. If the modern westerner judges their beauty or success by the standard of likeness to the shapes he knows in nature, he obviously must lose their own peculiar beauty. Naturalistic art (copied from nature) and derivative art (copied from other men's products) may of course be successful and be superficially lovely; but they can

[4]

never vie in perfection with the art of direct imagination of the sort that Europe produced in the past and Asia has nearly always produced.

Much of this Japanese sculpture is in human or nearly human shape and if we are to be scolded for using the familiar tests of naturalistic art and sound anatomy how then are we expected to enjoy and comprehend it?

First of all we must of course be willing and able to appreciate the use of symbols that are not our own. For us it is easy to accept the symbol of the Cross as being quite as expressive as if it were a picture or a statue of Christ in human form. But unfamiliar Buddhist symbols—a wheel or a lotus—we take to be actual representations of the things they most resemble. But a formal picture of a tree, after we have been told that it represents the Tree of Life, can be accepted in the west quite as readily as our own formal Tree of Jesse. It is even obvious that if it is too "good" (naturalistic) a picture of an oak or a poplar, that fact actually interferes with its success as a symbol. It might almost be said that the more formally or geometrically it is drawn or carved the more beautiful (perfect) it is as a symbol. From the formal Tree of Life, carved to represent an abstract idea, the step is an easy one to the formal use of the human body to represent abstract Buddhist deities. For these Oriental gods are not like our merely superhuman classical ones that can be labelled as Eros—human love or lust; Mars—warfare; Jupiter—the master; Mercury—the messenger; they are less definable, more abstract still; non-human rather than superhuman.

Thus when it is recognized that the Buddhist gods ought not to be represented as functioning biologically nor conforming to any standards of fleshly beauty, our minds are swept clear and are receptive. We are ready to see what beauty they may possess of their *own* kind.

This other beauty is of course that which is natural to the purpose for which they were made and the material out of which they have been fashioned; the special beauty of Buddhist abstractions and the special beauty of wood or stone, clay or bronze. These are brought out by the skill of the artist who carves or models the figure. His experience with the refractory stuff has taught him to model or to whittle shapes that shall be true to the material and shall serve adequately the purpose of religious symbols. Naturally the thing must be shaped into a recognizable symbol but it can not afford too close a resemblance to a human or other body. And it must be a beautiful (perfect) shape for wood or bronze or stone or clay.

If we love beautiful human bodies and can manage to fall in love with correct copies of them, that is fair enough. But few people would be so unreasonable as to ask the wood-carver to make a symbol for the benign abstraction called Amida which at the same time should imitate a lovely human youth. The reply to that request must of course be that lovely humanity can be no symbol for abstract divinity. The sculptor would add that his wooden statue, to be perfect, must not be humanly lovely but woodenly so.

All this may sound to western ears like some elaborately devised piece of special pleading to apologize for the clumsy oriental craftsmen ignorant of anatomy and unable to make convincing sculpture. But the test, in our case, is to examine, in that mood, the great religious sculpture of mediaeval Europe that was made before naturalistic and derivative forms had clouded our own symbols. The figures over the entrance to Chartres cathedral were not meant to function biologically. Judged as human beings they would be even repulsive. But what symbols in stone, what enrichment to that space on that building they are.

The Making of Statues

IT is a matter of prime importance to examine the methods by which these figures were made. To stare at them with no realizing sense of the materials and tools the craftsman deals with is to miss that comprehending pleasure with which one grasps why sliced wood has its peculiar beauties different from those inherent in poured bronze or in clay that is ductile under spatula and thumb.

BRONZE CASTING FROM WAX.   The making of bronze statues seems to have come to Japan with the Buddhist faith. The first casters were Koreans, lent from the nearby peninsula to practice their art and to teach it on the islands. Briefly, an image was modelled from wax and then covered with a thick layer of clay. The whole was then heated till the wax ran out through the vents left in the outer case. This hollow clay mould was then filled with moulten bronze that cooled precisely fitting its outer jacket, which was then chipped off. Such at least are the bare bones of the method. In practice it is a delicate and even an elaborate procedure.

HOLLOW IMAGES.   But it would be a wasteful, if not impossible, thing to make large images of solid metal. They must be hollow, with more or less thin walls. That was accomplished by modelling the wax about a core of clay that supported it. Over this thick wax layer, on which the craftsman had modelled his shapes, was now spread more clay through which vents and gates

[8]

were left for the hot wax to run out and the moulten metal to be poured in to take its place. The inner core and the outer shell, when the wax was gone from between them, must be braced apart by rods of cold metal soon to be surrounded by the moulten. The result, when the inner shapeless core of clay has been scooped out and the outer one chipped off, is a hollow figure made without waste or undue weight. So huge a thing as the great Buddha of Nara, some fifty-three feet high, could never have been made in this way. Only the head and the hands were cast as single shells of this sort. The rest was composed of slabs no less than six inches thick built up on edge. So too were the lotus petals of the throne on which it sits.

All this is worth dwelling on because of the emphasis it gives to the fact that bronze shapes are those of the modeller who builds up his stuff and pushes its facile surface about. But the shapes left by the knife that cuts wood away from rigid wood, or by the chisel that chips off stone, have quite other beauties and they are unique in those materials.

UNBAKED CLAY.   Statues of unbaked clay (*plates* 24, 25, 26) are found in the eighth century carried to the perfection of that technique, but none of importance remains from later times. It would seem as if the practice was soon abandoned. To make them, clay was moulded about a central armature of wood and its grip increased with the hair-like fibres of the wistaria roots; sometimes scraps of paper made of mulberry bark were also mixed in it. The final layers were made of a finer white clay so wet as to be laid on with a brush like thick paint. When the

[9]

figure dried, the surface was painted with a gesso-like mixture of china-clay with glue, which is particularly fitted to receive the final coat of colors. It will be seen that, in this form of sculpture, as in bronze, the surfaces are those of the modeller, never those of the carver. The great disadvantage was its weight and its fragility in large statues. No very free gesture of an unsupported arm or swing of drapery was possible in such friable stuff.

HOLLOW LACQUER SCULPTURE. A third technique of the Japanese modeller in the eighth century which did not later persist, was hollow lacquer. To make these statues, hemp cloths covered with the juice of the lacquer tree were draped and folded about a central armature (*plate* 16). When these stiffen as the juice dries, the result is a rigid light shell that can be tumbled about by earthquakes and suffer only surface scars easily repaired. Neither insects nor dry-rot nor moisture affect it nor is it, like bronze, subject to corrosion. In some cases, the technique for making heads and arms seems to have been varied by making shells of lacquered cloths, while they were still flexible, around a head or an arm modelled in clay. When the lacquer had set, the clay core was dug out. Such parts, made separately from the trunk, were then stitched to the body and the seams were hidden under layers of lacquered cloth. Small details, such as jewelry and hair, were added to the surface in paste made of lacquer stiffened with saw-dust or punk, to which a little powdered clay and rice-powder were added. This stuff adheres perfectly to its kindred surface and the whole takes gold leaf or color admirably.

No doubt these strong, light statues, sometimes more than life-size, were the result of the same demand which produces figures of paper stretched over bamboo framework to be carried in procession through the streets of India and China. In fact, certain scholars find in those the direct ancestors of the Japanese technique. Like many other things Japanese there is good evidence that lacquer sculpture originated in China, but there can be no denial that its real development is to be found in Japan.

DEVELOPMENT AND ABANDONMENT. Toward the end of the eighth century various modifications of the method were tried. Copper wire bound with twine was used for armatures in the fingers and parallel wires, with a web between to hold the lacquer, supported free drapery. It has never been satisfactorily explained why the art was abandoned for wood-carving in the early part of the tenth century. But one can watch the hollow shell giving gradual place to more or less completely detailed wooden cores, and lacquer becoming little more than a coating to preserve the surface and receive color. It is particularly instructive to watch this process of shifting emphasis from modelling to carving. For, as the one recedes and the other takes over control, their clear boundaries are for the moment blurred. Carved edges below seem but a support for cloths moulded with gum. Later, lacquered cloth masquerades in shapes proper only to the sliced grain of wood. But the craftsman's conscience soon wins and wood again becomes wood, with a mere paint film of lacquer to cover it.

WOOD CARVING. Last of all our processes I have put the cutting of wood, that it may be contrasted with the three kinds of modelling—clay, lacquer and bronze. Here is no docile substance like the others of a characterless structure. Stubborn, insisting on its own run of grain, sudden with knots, in the hands of a man who respects it wood helps the carver to unexpected beauties of line.

Although Japanese modellers of the eighth century have left us statues as glorious as any the world has produced in those other mediums, wood was perhaps, after all, what fitted the genius of the race. We see it persisting through the ages, shifting its shapes with the changes of fashion, flourishing, atrophying, decaying and then, of a sudden, alive with new purpose and fresh form under the knives of another generation. Down from the aloof Korean beauty of the Chuguji (*plates* 3 *and* 4) and the Yumeidono (*plates* 1 *and* 2) Kwannons, through the flowering of Nara times (*plates* 16 *to* 38), lapsing for a century, over-delicate for nearly three, we find statues in wood to charm us till Unkei, in the thirteenth century brings up the line with trumpets.

Suiko and Hakuho Periods

A.D. 552 to 710

IN the sixth century you are to imagine the people of the Japanese islands ripe and over-ripe for the high culture of China at their threshold. History seems to have no parallel of neighbors so unequal in civilization where the learner was as eager and as capable as Japan. Certainly there can be no comparison with contemporary barbarous England. For there Augustine was making his first Christian converts but the seven Saxon kingdoms were busy fighting among themselves and with the Celts, who were hardly below them in culture.

The first Buddhist missionaries that came to Japan brought a comparatively simple doctrine and required a limited hierarchy of images. It was to be another two centuries and a half before their multiplied profusion baulks the investigator, as it did the simple worshipper, with complicated ritual and questions of iconography. Before such problems occur it should be made clear that Buddhism was not, and never had been, either polytheist or pantheist. The separate deities of our own classical tradition, invoked each for his specialized supernatural power, might in certain aspects possibly be compared to the original Japanese Shinto religion, but they were remote from Buddhist belief. Nor, on the other hand, is it justifiable to label Buddhism pantheistic, as foreigners sometimes have done. The mere immanence, or identity, of deity with what we call natural phenomena was by no

[13]

means an Indian conception. Rather the Buddhist godhead was an Absolute, neither divisible nor to be thought of as mirrored in our world. Thus it will be seen that the various Buddhist gods, symbolized by the shapes of images with which this book is concerned, are but special aspects of the Whole Truth that man might presume to emphasize—never to separate.

Only the court circles and such Japanese statesmen and scholars as could use Chinese were at first accessible to the new faith or to the rest of the imported culture. Religious and philosophical ideas, theories of government and of behavior as well as laws and fashions of dress had at first the same source and the same limited patronage. And we shall see as they spread, that their importation was hardly under way before native genius modified all to native uses.

That the Japanese were never servile copyists in the matter of sculpture is amply proved by the fact that they succeeded in putting these new shapes to valid uses. And that, perhaps, is as much as the Romans or renaissance Europe did with what they borrowed from the Greeks. Some of the earliest sculptures in Japan were imported from Korea or China, but for the most part they were made on Japanese soil by foreign craftsmen and their native apprentices. The style of these sculptures was already familiar on the continent, but since these are more beautiful, and some are unique, they have peculiar importance to us; first because of their singular beauty and second, because certain types at least are not represented by Chinese or Korean examples. Buddhist persecutions and the demand for copper coin caused the larger bronzes

[14]

in China to be melted up, nor have examples of early wood and clay survived. For our knowledge of continental styles we must depend entirely on numerous small bronzes and on the splendid rock-cut statues in cliff-chapels. But, happily, Japan has preserved a few large bronzes of great importance, some three score smaller ones and over a dozen priceless woods, in addition to the wooden carvings that embellish the canopies of Horyuji temple at Nara.

It is significant that all this remaining material is Buddhist. No carved household gear or lay decoration is left, and there was probably little enough of it in the early years. The statues owe their preservation to their sacred character and to the fact that some of their temples are still standing.

It is obvious that these symbolic figures were meant to be immediately comprehended by the devout. Incarnate Buddha—Shaka—in his monk's robe, represented the summit of the Unattainable toward which man yearns. It was hardly more definite than that. The several Bodhisattva, as has been pointed out, were differently prized for certain attributes of that godhead and were to be invoked for benefits—Health (*Yakushi*), Wisdom (*Monju*), Mercy (*Jizo* and *Miroku*). The subsidiary figures were but guardians of the gate, guardians of the inner shrine, choirs of heavenly beings and the immediate disciples of the historic Buddha during his stay on earth. These lesser ones have merely superhuman, rather than non-human, powers or are subordinate attendants.

The volcanic islands produce little stone that is fit for the sculptor's chisel. Thus, in contrast to contemporary China, the statues of Japan had to be of clay, bronze or wood. No rock cliffs like those that line the Chinese rivers gave the Japanese a chance to excavate cave-chapels after the continental fashion or enrich their walls with painted reliefs hewn out of the mother-rock. From the very first the images were, therefore, conceived in wood or bronze in the full round to be set on central altars where the liturgists pace and circle. The walls were painted in flat tempera colors with tall deities grouped in paradise.

Tempyo or Nara Period

A.D. 710 TO 794

By A.D. 710 the new foreign forces had been already some years in increasing operation, though by no means smoothly adjusted to native conditions. But at least it could be said that there was no longer any doubt that China had been accepted as mentor by the Japanese. The Imperial House no longer set up fresh palaces and seats of government with each new reign, but settled at the western end of Nara city which was being laid out in rectangular avenues and streets after the fashion of the Chinese capitals.

As we look back on the next seventy-five years, the effect produced is of a people intent on nothing so much as the acquirement of Chinese civilization in every aspect. The problem of language was being partially solved, in its written form at least, by rendering Japanese words in the medium of the Chinese written characters. Confucianism was taught as the main vehicle for Chinese culture and the legal code of the T'ang dynasty was more or less thoroughly accepted. Court dress, manners, amusements, social and intellectual standards, the calendar, the arts of medicine, war and teaching—all were Chinese.

The fundamental soundness of the culture thus sought out by the Japanese and the broad reasonableness of the new religion can be examined in high relief against the background of Nearer Eastern history in those same years. It was precisely then that

[17]

the propagation of Mahometan culture was at its full height. "The Koran, tribute, or death." Persia, Palestine, Syria, Jerusalem, Antioch, Damascus. Ctesiphon with all its riches, Persepolis and Merv—Mother of Cities, all were being sacked. And the library of Alexandria was afire.

But the Far East was a different picture. Two generations had barely passed before continental culture from China was being practiced on the islands of Japan as the definite goal for a whole nation. And indeed China of the T'ang dynasty is accepted to have been by far the most civilized country of the contemporary world. Nothing in that time of the west equalled T'ang in art, letters, science and urbane living. The Buddhist sculpture, which is what concerns us, forms an excellent mirror for what was stirring. Native apprentices from the work-shops set up in Japan by imported Chinese and Korean master-craftsmen were becoming masters in their own right. Preserving every jot of their teachers' skill, they lent to continental shapes and styles something that we shall, as soon as the eighth century reaches its second decade, recognize as peculiarly Japanese.

It would, however, be to miss entirely the real significance of those swift and crowded years to assume that the Nara culture was a lifeless, or even a correct, copy of the continental. Practices that did not fit the Japanese habit of mind were discarded or modified till they should do so. Sometimes the change was deliberate, but more often a keen and busy people unconsciously pushed the model aside in favor of their own fresh and original development. That the new form was often thought to be Chinese

[18]

by its Japanese inventors proves how earnestly the islanders were at work on self-education.

As it was with intellectual processes so it was with sculpture. The collossal rock-sculptures cut in the cliff, which the Japanese pilgrims to China had seen, were of course impossible to emulate in a volcanic country. But a bigger bronze one, sheltered in a larger wooden temple than the world had ever seen, was now begun. Forty years after the Nara capital had been established this was successfully cast and the *Daibutsu-den*, its temple, was finished.

All during this time the capital had been a hive of activity, preparing for the great event. The copper supply of the Empire was nearly drained to pour into the gigantic moulds and all the gold then available was exhausted for the gilding. Scores of new temples and thousands of new priests all over the country were being supplied with all the liturgical accessories. Robes of cotton and brocade were being woven, whole libraries of holy books were laboriously copied out by scribes. Bells and candlesticks and everywhere paintings and images and more images were being made.

So great a number of statues of enduring perfection could never have been produced if the sculptor's craft had not already passed largely into native hands. Chinese and Koreans still designed and supervised, but the pupils had become adept and, in many cases, entirely competent to work alone. If this had not been true, the Nara period would not stand out today as the short century of Far Eastern sculpture that is comparable with the very greatest,

east or west. If this had been the work of copyists, lit by no very
special vital flame, later generations of Japanese artists could
never have developed from it such noble and consistent styles as
this picture-book shows.

Jogan Period

A.D. 794 to 897

TODAY no man can tell precisely what happened to send the court and the seat of government packing off to Nagaoka in 784 and then to the banks of the Kamo river, some thirty miles off at Kyoto. That move had a definite, if superficial, effect on the look of the sculpture of the time. For the six great monastic establishments remained behind at the old capital and did not, by any means, transfer their work-shops and their image-makers with the court. Hence there comes a break in the style of wood-carving that, to some extent, may be accounted for by new workmen and other traditions.

INTRODUCTION OF MYSTIC SECTS. But a far more fundamental reason for the new style can be traced in the introduction of new requirements from the Buddhist church which was then, as always, the patron. Two promising young men, Dengyo Daishi and Kobo Daishi, had received grants to study in China and were now, at the beginning of the ninth century, back in Kyoto the new capital. To Dengyo was allotted Mount Hiye, which stands over the northeast of the city, and there he built his monastery and training school for monks, called Enryakuji. He devoted himself to the doctrines of the *Tendai* sect which, for all its Chinese origin, proved singularly apt for the conditions and mentality of that day in Japan. Kobo Daishi created another great monastic school on Mount Koya to the south of Nara. This

[21]

was more remote from the capital by some four or five days' journey, but it was none the less powerful in its effect on Japanese intellectual life. Here the emphasis was on the doctrines of *Shingon*—the True Word. Both sects were strongly mystical, both emphasized ritual words and gestures and demanded images to be made to represent a multiplicity of deities hitherto unknown in Japan. A plain man could no longer deal direct with the host of god-names into which the old godhead was now subdivided. He must approach through the medium of paid priests. These made it a life-work to untangle the iconography. The new images acquired multiple arms and faces and attributes to such an extent that the mere sight of them suggested how much magical procedure of incantation and of mystic gesture must be learned by rote. True, the native gods, who since the beginning had haunted their familiar shrines beloved of villagers, were often now associated with the Indian Buddhist divinities as special shapes which the visiting gods had deigned to occupy. But the human appeal thus gained for Buddhism, by combination with the better-known gods, was largely wasted when an unfamiliar mysticism made them seem more remote. Common people approached god less simply and only through a tangled thicket of esoteric practices that discouraged all but professional initiates.

FEW BRONZES AND CLAYS. NO DRIED LACQUER.   For reasons not understood today, bronze sculpture suffers a partial eclipse and hollow lacquer and clay seem to have been entirely abandoned. Of wood there are a few glorious examples left from this period (*plates* 36 *to* 38). But there are also a number of less skillful

[22]

ones that show how the break with the Nara craftsmen had caused a definite decline. It seems, to western eyes at least, that progress in the carver's art was set back and that something had been forgotten that must be painstakingly learnt again. The result, in general, can be said to be clumsier work by men who were less at home in their material. Features and drapery in such statues seem but one removed from drawing on the log. However, none of this less satisfactory class has been chosen for illustration in a book designed rather for immediate pleasure than for teaching. In fact a foreigner properly hesitates to dismiss off-hand the output of three generations of honest craftsmen whose work may not happen to be to his taste. Especially I hesitate to do this in view of the affection in which I hold the examples of Jogan sculpture here shown. (For instance *plate* 38). This statue is headless and has been stripped of arms and feet and color, but it remains integral and moving none the less and it is one of my most striking examples of the supremacy of Japanese carving.

Fujiwara Period

A.D. 897 TO 1185

MANY scholars engaged on the history of Japanese art dwell rather lightly on the sculpture of the Fujiwara epoch—the tenth and twelfth centuries. No very large number of examples remains and what is left, on superficial examination, is perhaps suggestive of the rigid formulas that were in force. The Yamato schools of painting, which began to blossom at the end of the period, show a fresh and native virtue, literature provides one of the greatest novels known (*The Tale of Genji*) and the alluring sophistication of court manners, irresistible to the historian, all have distracted our attention from the important subject of wood-carving. Bronze seems to have been less frequently used and hollow lacquer and unbaked clay quite disappeared.

NATIONALIZATION AND DIGESTION. With no fresh impulses from the continent Japan, forced to employ what former years had brought, at last found free rein for her national genius. The formalism demanded by esoteric Buddhism united with the urbanity of a sophisticated court to produce shapes that were feminine and suave. But it must be remembered that craftsmen were still governed by their old canons of purpose and material and by their own vivid mental image of what had to be made. Wood was not yet tortured out of its valid shapes nor did artists presume to dictate to church or court what they must think lovely. The time for loose individualism and of art for art's sake was, happily, not

[24]

yet. Artists sought, as always, the perfection of what they made rather than to express themselves or to copy nature. Within the strict canons of church requirements, however, we see, with relief, the appearance of an increasing range of subject matter. The very names of gods were now become legion and each was different from the others in attitude and attributes. It was the various conceptions of the godhead that were being variously emphasized, and the result was a multiplication of image-forms and their appropriate rituals.

A SIMPLER BUDDHISM.   Things had reached such a state by the early eleventh century that the very sects—Tendai and Shingon—which had kept their inner doctrine hidden from the layman must develop their own corrective in a form of protestantism that would provide direct contact with the deity. Indian thought of eight centuries before gave precedent for this and the idea had also been developed by the Chinese to a certain degree; Amida, Lord of Illimitable Light, actually came from his western paradise to save the individual. His effulgence could be seen. Even good works were no longer necessary that the true believer should be saved. To call on the name of Amida (*Namu Amida Butsu*) was enough. Thus the principle of personal struggle, or the doctrine of works, soon yielded to reliance on god.

PARADISE SCENES.   This conception, new to Japan, demanded new shapes of images. The change was first noticeable in paintings which showed the Amida with his hosts descending from the clouds to take up the human soul. The gracious composition implied in such pictures gave scope for a fresh and human

[25]

treatment that developed into an apt vehicle for the almost feminine elaboration of those times. Sculpture followed as well as might be, even to the setting up of elaborate carved groups expressing this same scene. Dramatically arranged sets of figures had been known in Buddhist sculpture as early as those groups of clay statuettes at the beginning of the eighth century and five centuries earlier in Chinese cave sculpture. But such compositions were, from their very nature, easier to produce in painting, where they were map-like diagrams of Sanscrit symbols or formally rendered pictures of enthroned deities in paradise. Sculpture being difficult and costly to make in groups, the single figure of Amida was usually enough to symbolize him. The main change in style lies in the welcoming attitude and gesture.

CUT GOLD LEAF.   We have seen that the Japanese sculptors had, before this, perfected several of the techniques which they received from the continent and that they had surpassed their masters in using them. They had, for instance, made splendid use of hollow lacquer and of clay and had developed unprecedented skill as carvers in wood. They had also developed a thinner stronger gesso to be spread under the color on all statues except bronze. Another interesting technical process now appears, probably borrowed from the makers of sacred paintings but, so far as is known, originating in Japan. It is worth dwelling on for the gradual superficial change that it produced in the look of late Fujiwara sculpture and for the fact that it has been used as one of the chief mechanical tests for dating statues of the late Fujiwara and Kamakura periods. Not content with the comparatively dusty appearance of gold powder mixed with glue on the surfaces of their figures, gold leaf was actually laid down on the surface over a thin animal glue. Large areas had presented little difficulty, but very thin lines and patterns had not hitherto been possible. In Europe the method was to lay down a thin line of varnish, or other adhesive, with gold leaf above. When the leaf was firmly fixed excess gold, beyond the areas of the line, could be dusted off. The result was indeed a fine line, fitted to the scale of the illuminated miniatures. The Japanese method was more elaborate and gave a slightly different character to the resulting line. The gold leaf was laid on a buckskin pad and cut with a knife made from one of the innumerable varieties of Japanese bamboo, one that was found not to tear but sever the leaf clean. It was not long before this delicate craft was elaborated to an almost incredibly minute detail. Leaf was folded according to an intricate scheme (like the rows of paper dolls, hand-in-hand, we cut out with scissors) and, when sliced with a calculated economy of cuts, it was opened out to show a lace-like web. This web was laid down on lines of wet glue and it suggested brocade on the Amida's robe. When, during the thirteenth century, the glittering mesh shone over a matt surface of powdered gold, the result was particularly rich. A fine angularity of shape, inherent in the pattern produced by a knife on metal leaf, sometimes saved from sentimentality a figure that had been carved in the mellifluous surfaces of decadent times.

Kamakura Period

A.D. 1185 to 1336

CHANGE OF TEMPORAL POWER.   When Yoritomo, the Generalissimo, set up his court and camp three hundred miles northeast of Kyoto to rule in the name of the Emperor, political and social conditions underwent a radical change. The two hundred years during which direct power was exercised from the new city are called by its name—Kamakura.

The old manner of statue-making continued, weaker and continually less important, for alongside it had sprung up a fresh manner and new techniques. These are infused with so vital a spirit as to produce a body of deathless sculpture that entirely outshines the dying old flame. The Imperial court at Kyoto, sucked dry of direct power, of funds and of statesmen was, like the outworn artistic tradition, half-forgotten in the zest for new life. Let us see what the changed patronage for sculpture was, and what fresh ideas were now clamoring for expression in every artistic medium. The thing can be got at only through some knowledge of the intellectual and emotional changes that were taking place in the Buddhism of that day.

PURE LAND SECTS.   We have seen the doctrines of an easy paradise preached during the latter days of the Fujiwara epoch and already established ten years before the military government was set up in Kamakura. People were sick of the old Tendai and Shingon Buddhism by which no layman could approach god. But

[28]

for all that, Honen, the preacher of a reformed simplicity, was reviled and exiled by the establishment, for he struck at the very root of priest-craft and of comfortable livings. When he was re-called at the popular demand, he died with the praise of Amida on his lips, convinced his prayer was enough.

The method of final salvation that I have taught is neither a sort of meditation such as that practiced by many scholars in China and Japan in the past, nor is it a repetition of the Buddha's name by those who have studied and under-stood the deep meaning of it. It is nothing but the mere repetition of the name of the Buddha Amida without a doubt of his mercy, whereby one may be born into the Land of Perfect Bliss. (Sansom, *Japan*, p.321)

PURE LAND SHINSHU DOCTRINES.   The next logical step in the same direction came when these Pure Land doctrines were taken up to be carried on by the monk Shonin. He began where Honen left off and evolved a theory that Amida's mercy is so illimitable that one may safely forego the difficult act of faith in pronouncing the invocation *Namu Amida Butsu*. The words alone were potent to secure rebirth in paradise. This doctrine spread like wildfire and millions today practice it. Their clergy are not even celibate, but they encourage morality and manage the huge endowments that have flowed in to their foundations.

REFORMS OF NICHIREN.   Somewhat later in the period, Ni-chiren preached in the streets of Kamakura against this loose Amidism and against the ancient monasticism that still held at Nara. His formula for invoking heaven was a similar one, but it was addressed to the Lotus of the Good Law and was not cal-culated to secure immediate unconditional paradise. The doctrine

[29]

was more often than not couched in terms of bitter abuse of other tenets and was charged with nationalistic and political significance. The warriors of Kamakura, busy with constructing an entirely new social framework, from tax-levies to foreign relations, were caught by a creed that could be turned to their immediate interest. Honen and Shonin had concerned themselves with paradise, but here in the streets was a popular orator insisting on reforms and the punishment of rebels against state and church— all to the beat of drums. There are millions of Nichiren's followers today, and it may be that this thirteenth century creed gives us a hint for the comprehension of modern Japan. But how, it may be asked, does all this affect the styles in sculpture? One more main Buddhist movement must be summarized, however briefly, before the background has been set to examine the new forms in art.

THE CREED OF ZEN.   Zen, the third form of Buddhism to be considered in connection with the sculptures of the Kamakura epoch, had an effect on style in art deep-seated and obvious enough to be demonstrated. Its philosophical content, however, may take a man's whole thinking life to master. In English Dr. Suzuki has devoted several most illuminating volumes to the subject and Sansom's history contains a remarkable summary for beginners. He writes in part:

It is at first sight surprising that the vigorous society of Kamakura should have patronized a sect usually described as contemplative. But Zen has other than contemplative qualities. Its principles were at an early date in China summed up in the following lines:

[30]

"A special transmission outside the scriptures,

No dependence on the written word,

Direct pointing at the soul of man,

Seeing one's nature and attaining Buddhahood.

It will be seen that even on simple, practical grounds there was much in Zen to appeal to a soldier, particularly one of a self-reliant character. Zen does not depend upon scriptures, it has no elaborate philosophy; it is indeed almost anti-philosophical in that it stresses the importance of a realization of truth which comes as a vision due to introspection and not to the study of other men's words. To feudal warriors of the sternest type, the emotionalism of the Pure Land sects must have been distasteful, and they were no doubt impatient of the metaphysical subtleties of the other schools. Most of them, for that matter, were not learned enough to comprehend their difficult terminology. But the sudden enlightenment, called *satori*, at which a Zen practicioner aims, is an intimate personal experience. A Zen teacher reads no sutras, he performs no ceremonies, worships no images, and he conveys instruction to his pupil not by long sermons but by hints and indications. The pupil must examine himself, master himself and find his own place in the spiritual universe by his own efforts. So incommunicable is Zen that it has no canon . . . " (Sansom, p.330)

ANTI-ARTISTIC CONDITIONS.   To recapitulate with an eye for the stimulus afforded our craft: we have the Pure Land sects promising paradise, incontinent, to the believer who calls on Amida. Next the Shinshu doctrines also claiming their thousands who were not required even the effort of belief if they would but consent to repeat the verbal formula. Third comes Nichiren's reform of earlier Shingon, also scorning magic apparatus (art). Lastly, in Zen, is a definite refusal of all gear that might come between man and his identity with god.

[31]

To dwell on what would seem such artless phases of the Buddhist church during the thirteenth century is but to emphasize the unconquerable instinct for art among the Japanese, the instinct that surmounted all obstacles. As a matter of fact, fresh and lively forms were now created to the admiration of all later times, and they came into being under the unpromising patronage described. The explanation, therefore, can not lie in the obvious tenets of the new creeds but in the attitude of the people toward them. The new style of sculpture might be shaped to conform to Pure Land Buddhism or to the teachings of Nichiren, but it is always flavored with Zen. Zen, convinced that paraphernalia such as images and even sacred books are barriers to comprehension, made much of the direct and communicable personality of its leaders. Even though their sermons were not written down and they worked "by hints and indications", the spirit that informed these men must not be lost. Hence portraiture. For there is no danger of mistaking the seeming flesh of a wrinkled old monk for pure Buddhist enlightenment, but everyone who had seen that monk would recall something of his flame. Here in literal portraiture no idolatry should slip in. Further, the Buddha and the myriad Bodhisattva are of the very same essence as the blade of grass or of the dew that is on it and fresh emphasis on such natural forms should stand for better, cleaner symbols to evoke god than images in the old hieratic half-human shape.

A study of the painting of the day makes this tendency obvious at once. But even sculpture, a craft less sensitive than painting to swift impression by sketch or fleeting mood, kept nobly up.

[32]

Among the masterpieces of wood-carving of the time is Kuya Shonin (*plates* 64 *and* 65), his gong hung on his breast and in his right hand the mallet to sound it. In his left hand is the famous staff tipped with stag-horn with which he belabored his heretics. The figure is a lean, old-young man with rapt visage carved in a manner so life-like as to startle one. It seems like a contradiction to all we have learnt of Buddhist symbolism in sculpture. Formerly sculptors dared not insist on human likeness for very fear of losing divinity, now comes scrupulous recording of the shapes that are observed which, of course, are not divine. But the easy pleasure a westerner may take in it is a trap. For here indeed is a symbol, but of a new sort. Instead of being but one step removed from the abstraction of deity it is two steps removed. The old closed circle has a wider radius, but still it is perfect and returns on itself to god. It now reads:

— abstract god —

— a formula to bring man to god —

— an old man crying the formula in the streets —

— abstract god — .

To return to the image. Suddenly with strange and rather horrid insistence (in western eyes) out from the mouth pop a row of little images of Amida. Surely it was not necessary thus to carve in wood symbols of the words which in themselves are but symbols. This leaves little, even for a dull imagination, to ponder. And yet when we have recovered from the unaccustomed sight, that lean old figure remains as vivid as any sculpture or painting of John the Baptist from our own High Renaissance.

It would never do to be too ingenious in one's attempts to explain what seems to be an influx of realism into the sculptor's art. But there can be no doubt that it was due, as has been said, in some degree to the common-sense attitude of Zen Buddhism and its consequent emphasis on individual character. Once the artists' feet were set toward realism and toward portraiture it was a temptation to go farther. Thus we find them indulging for the first time in such experiments as carving their sacred figures in the nude, to be dressed up later as we dress dolls, in actual clothes. But until we know more of this matter, and of the esoteric meanings later ascribed to such statues, we must account for it as the mere effervescence of the successful craftsman seeking fresh outlets and cheerfully tackling—even creating—mechanical difficulties.

KOKEI'S PUPILS.   Tradition still lives that two apprentices worked at the same bench in the Kyoto image-shop of Kokei the master-carver just after the middle of the twelfth century. Their names were Unkei and Kaikei and they were, respectively, son and nephew of the master who trained them rigorously in the tradition that had come to him direct from Jocho his famous ancestor. Kaikei the nephew followed this traditional path, and when he had worked out his apprenticeship he made statues in his own Kyoto shop that differed from those of his forebears only by being more beautiful.

1000-ARMED KWANNONS.   Within the last few years it has been definitely established that it was from this Kyoto workshop that the thousand-armed Kwannon and its scores of thousand-armed attendants were produced for the Sanjusangen-do—the thirty-three span temple. They stand in serried rows down the long hall and one looks at them in the shadows aghast at the labor implied by their very number and elaboration. To the westerner it seems inevitable that any man, or group of men, setting about the task of carving such images will deliberately or insensibly skimp the pains necessary to make all the statues, all the arms, all the hands and all the fingers perfect. But the westerner would be wrong. To prove how wrong he is I show on *plate* 52 a single example from among the smallest, most numerous and least conspicuous of the hands. Among the scores that I have taken pains to examine none was inferior to this. It was a great tradition, worthily upheld.

UNKEI.   But Unkei, the son of the master, not content merely to sustain the tradition, was as great an innovator as the warriors and philosophers who employed him. His name sounds in Japanese ears as the name of Michelangelo sounds in our own. In spite of this great fame—or because of its myth-making quality—we know little of his actual life. We come on him first, at the top of his bent, carving the astonishing woods that stand vigorous and distinct apart from the whole fifteen centuries of Japanese Buddhist sculpture. It is therefore of uncommon interest to learn that Unkei, like the greatest artists in every age, was deeply concerned with the mechanics of his craft. In fact in his case "mere" carpentry made it possible to achieve his ultimate beauty. Futher, it was a determining factor in the new naturalism and in portraiture. He is credited with inventing an entirely new system of joinery to make his figures. This was logical and, as we shall see, calculated to aid the carver in every stage of his task. Perhaps its greatest use was to set free the mind of the sculptor from the restrictions of shape imposed by log and plank and block.

LIMITATIONS OF EARLY METHODS.   In the eighth and ninth centuries the tree, even before it was felled, suggested the tall cylindrical statue that was hidden within it; and when the statue was done it recalled the tree. Lines and channels had been scored the length of the log, more or less deeply, for drapery. Shoulders had been squared off and the blockhead left, still attached. Arms were then added and, where the toes of a standing figure jutted beyond the limits of a tree-bole, those too were added. But the log had always constrained the artist and limited his conception and his formal idea.

UNKEI'S INVENTIONS.   Later a technique was elaborated that proved slightly more adaptable but was not essentially different. Seated figures especially, consisted in a thick block for the lap pushed up against a log which was the trunk and head. But now, in Unkei's workshop, log and slab were no longer master. To make one statue, dozens of curiously shaped smaller units, planned according to an elaborate geometry, were separately roughed out by apprentices to scale from the master's small patterns. Overseers assembled these unpromising blocks and slabs into a hollow pyramid that should be the statue. On this were marked the incurves to be hollowed and the protuberances to be spared. When these were separately carved, and all joints fitted true, the hollow pile was again set up and double-pronged staples

[36]

of iron clamped the blocks close. Free hanging drapery, and that which hugs the figure, was added in long strips tapering cleverly to nothing where cloth should seem tight against the body. It will be readily seen how the schematic preparation of these various blocks and shapes, to be glued and clamped together, made it not only possible but necessary to delegate the early stages to apprentices. Also that, in doing so, there was no loss of the master's original conception. His was the plan and when, before its final stage, the built-up figure came back to his hands roughed out it came precise in scale and proportion, needing but his touches to make it perfect. If an error had been made in an earlier detail that block was easily removed and another shaped to fill its place.

SHAPING THE HEAD.   In making the head the original timber-end, and later the separate block that was sunk between the shoulders, had been done away with some century and a half before Unkei. Already the practice in his father's workshop was to scoop out a thick mask and a thick occiput and to glue them together back of the ears. But Unkei still further refined the method. His heads were divided in three, the mask, the hollow ring on the edges of which were the ears and, lastly, the occiput. When he held this light mask, with its square blocked-out features, in his hand to shape it, unlimited new possibilities were immediately obvious to the carver. It was no longer a solid knob at the end of a prone post about which he must circle with mallet and chisel or, at best, straddle to reach. Nor was it a fifteen-pound block at which he must hack. The shell-like mask was too delicate

[37]

to take or need the shocks of a mallet. In his very hand he turned it about and observed where shadows fell, or he held it at arm's length and saw where a groove must be deeper. Half-finished, he set it on his proper shoulders to judge the angle and, while it was not changing shape under his knife, it hung in the workshop for leisured study at the desired height. Likeness to life, with this intimate handling, became his interest. Portraiture was in the thing. No wonder now that even his high gods and his half-gods, for sheer joy in the new ability, showed a close observation of life that had never before even tempted the Buddhist carver.

Much has been made by Japanese art historians of the contribution to portraiture made by Zen Buddhism. But I wonder if the improved mechanics that brought easy handling of the visage, and made the medium more sensitive, were not even more responsible than philosophy for the change. But there was, with the quickening of the obvious spirit, a corresponding loss of the abstract symbol.

Unkei was sent from Kamakura to Nara by the Shogun and he set up his workshop at Todaiji monastery which had been burnt in the civil wars a decade before. Luckily there were still left in the vicinity a score or more eighth century statues more or less undamaged. The chance to study these masterpieces and occasionally to restore their missing parts, seems to have had great influence on the style of Unkei and his group. It would never have occured to them to copy, but sheer craftsman's respect for their predecessors' skill forbade introducing any jarring note.

[38]

FEWER MODELLERS THAN CARVERS. It has yet to be explained why the modelling of clay or of dried lacquer was little used at this time, or not at all. What is left of eighth century sculpture suggests that modelling was at that time as common as woodwork and one would have expected to find plenty of modelling remaining from Unkei's stay at Nara in the thirteenth century.

CHINESE BRONZE CASTERS. It is true that modellers for bronze were brought over from China of the contemporary Sung dynasty. Chin Wa kei and his brother Chin Ju, with their workmen, had been invited to Nara at this time in order to model and replace the head melted from the shoulders of the Dai Butsu statue when its great temple was burnt. But one is permitted to doubt if their contribution was particularly significant. Certainly it was not comparable with that which had been made to Japanese art by their compatriots five centuries before when they had cast the first edition of that same head. But whatever the inferiority of this second head, it must have been immeasurably superior to the third, the one we now see on those clumsy shoulders. In making delicate bronzes the Sungs were undoubtedly great, but there is no dateable Buddhist sculpture from China in any medium of their time that does not show decline.

North and South Period

(NAMBOKU CHO) A.D. 1336 TO 1392

WOOD-CARVING—and there are few sculptures from this period in any other medium—in spite of the civil wars retains something of the strength of Kamakura times. It was, however, noticeably mollified to an urbanity and a convention imposed on it by the return of social headquarters to Kyoto the former capital. In reality the century was anything but urbane. Rival branches of the Imperial House set the great families at each other's throats and the land was ravaged. The destruction of works of art in burning monasteries and castles amounted to a national calamity. Though the real government was again in Kyoto the picture of that ancient seat of culture was a distressing one.

Here were the usual fruits of war, the "sudden Lords" (*niwaka daimyo*) uneasy in their court dress, the penniless soldiers pawning their armour, the hectic search for pleasure, the extremes of profusion and want. The successful warriors, while treating the court nobles with contempt, aspired to their breeding and their elegance. Yoritomo's vassals had been strictly and of set purpose segregated from the aristocrats, but now many great feudal families from eastern and western Japan had their residences in Kyoto. There was the Shogun's palace in Muromachi, and nearby it the mansions of the Hosokawa, the Shiba, the Yamana and such-like chieftains, where they revelled in the intervals of their campaigns. (Sansom, *Japan*, p.344)

Ashikaga Period

A.D. 1392 to 1568

PEACE AND ART.   But once the Imperial succession was settled the arts of peace, stunted but never actually cut off, were eagerly resumed. The Ming dynasty had been on the Chinese throne for a quarter of a century and trade with them (to the Chinese it was always "tribute") started briskly up. Copper cash were brought in bulk to the islands along with the coveted brocades and medicines and pig-iron. In return went the flawless sword-blades which the Japanese had long been forging to the despair of the continent, sulphur from the volcanoes, lacquer table-ware superior to that of south China and the folding fans that seem to have been a Japanese invention.

CHINESE IMPORTS.   Owing partly to the fact that the great religious houses of Japan invested in this trade, to the extent of even fitting out cargo-boats bearing the names of the monasteries, we find in those centres an immediate influx of Chinese ideas and works of art. But it must be carefully noted, as further proof of Japanese discrimination, that it was the art of a former, not the contemporary, Chinese dynasty that seized their imagination. If sculpture was too bulky or not good enough to be imported in quantity, the paintings and writings of past generations were secured for Japan by the hundred. In particular the works of the Sung dynasty ink-painters expressed the taste of the Japanese Zenists to a nicety. Chinese art under the Mings was, for the

[41]

moment, on another tack, and these early treasures or copies of them could be secured even at the ports. The representation of nature with a mystic content and a Zen point of view was now so widely practiced in Japan and with so masterly a skill that it might be said that the Sung renaissance took place on the islands rather than in its native land of China.

It is amusing, though not in the least significant, to remember that the precise contemporaries in Europe of these delicate Shoguns who were the greatest collectors and patrons of art Japan has known, who had at their court painters and poets and who were advised by the learned men of the church and who rejoiced in their great garden-villas, were none other than the Medici in Florence. But Kyoto knew nothing of Italy, nor Florence of Japan in spite of Marco Polo.

But it was painting and philosophy and architecture that were thus refreshed and stimulated from abroad. Sculpture, which is our subject, was far less amenable to new ideas. True, carving was still admirable in Japan, but little enough of that time remains, and the best of what is left often seems but an adequate if sometimes frigid modernization of Kamakura. There are half a dozen portrait statues of priests and nobles (*plates* 60 *to* 63) in which one sees, topping an almost cubistic mound of mediaeval garments, skull and visage portrayed to the very life and afire with character. I do not know, however, that the carving of purely Buddhist images can be said to have preserved the old skill or meaning. Certainly there was no Unkei.

Zen Buddhism that we have watched while it infused the sculptural forms, even of other sects, neglected our medium during the twelfth and thirteenth centuries for the quicker abstractions of ink painting. In this connection it will be noticed that portraits in wood bear so close a resemblance to those on paper—both in composition and line—that hasty observers have called the sculpture calligraphic. No wood-carver would so consider it. He would find in Ashikaga carvings a far better conception of bulk in three dimensions than in the work of any Japanese or Chinese image-makers before the Kamakura period. That drapery edges were sharply rendered, as with a brush, is rather the result of the realistic sense than of a slavish adherence to the mannerisms of a different technique. In the earlier centuries of wood in Japan, and of stone in China, the lines first sketched on the surface of the log or stone did in fact influence the carver, and his work was then more truly calligraphic in its failure to conceive in the round.

DRAMA MASKS.   A single and most obvious exception to all the above generalities about Ashikaga sculpture and its possible failure to kindle fresh fires was the art of the carver of masks for the use of the *No* drama (*plate* 70). Constructed to hide the face of the actor in the almost liturgical posturing dances, these light wooden masks will rank among the greatest that have ever been produced. The seventh and eighth centuries had dance masks of another sort (*plate* 35). Those were false heads to be used on high platforms in the open sun or in the glare of torches. But these false faces of Ashikaga and later years were used indoors. They are carved with a subtle contrivance of simplicity which seems perhaps the summit of calculated restraint in sculpture. The elder

[43]

half-gods and demons were rugged and course and grotesque. These are sleek with a deceptive vacuity which must be watched moving on the stage to be comprehended.

Momoyama Period

A.D. 1568 to 1615

CIVIL WARS.   Historians mark off the Momoyama period as an arbitrary limit for certain important and cultural innovations. But if sculptural styles are to be our narrow criterion we should prolong those significant years till 1638 when Japan was definitely closed against foreign influences and there was leisure again, as from the ninth to the twelfth centuries, to digest. Almost incessant fighting by no means killed art but there can be no doubt that it, together with other influences, shifted the emphasis away from temple images.

NEW ARISTOCRACY.   In the middle of the sixteenth century came the civil wars that toppled all the ancient baronial houses. Up from their ruins rose an entirely different patronage for art under the great General Nobunaga who served the last puppet Ashikaga Shogun and then usurped his power. A common soldier in Nobunaga's forces, Hideyoshi, rose from the ranks to become his ablest general and his successor with the title of Taiko—Generalissimo. His palace at Momoyama, half a dozen miles from Kyoto, was long ago levelled but it provides a title for this short epoch and is a name in men's mouths for splendor. If Hideyoshi was no exquisite it may at least be said of him that he learned to be a better patron of the arts than ever his contemporary upstart, Cromwell, could have been.

When Nobunaga was murdered (two years before Raleigh

[45]

landed in Virginia) Hideyoshi and Tokugawa Ieyasu carried on the campaign to unify the country. The latter was destined to found the Shogunate that lasted till the coming of Perry's black ships. This campaign was so perfect a success that the two leaders were soon able to turn their attention to China and Korea. In the peninsula they made a nominal conquest that was marked in the history of art by the transfer of Korean craftsmen to Japan and a consequent remarkable stimulus to Japanese applied art, particularly to pottery.

ARCHITECTURAL CARVING. Sculptured images were of course still supplied for the spoiled and almost depopulated monasteries. But it will be noticed that this brief book illustrates none of these. Rather we must emphasize the fact that sculptors in wood turned largely to the embellishment of the palaces of the *nouveaux riches*. The depth and significance of this trend can be clearly seen only when it is examined against the background of the delicate times that were past. For then we saw a painstaking elimination of the obvious by artists who were poets and wits and mystics. Now the forthright soldier had become the patron of taste and he must have his gold leaf by the acre. No wit or allusion or subtleness could live in these abrupt and obvious times. Carvers now embellished the overdoors of palaces (*plates* 71 *to* 73) and of palatial temples with such intricacy of colored shapes that one stands in amazement to gape. They reached a facility that, by another generation, proved their downfall. It then became an end in itself to be clever. Embellishment hid structure. But that time did not come immediately and, during the first three decades of

[46]

the seventeenth century, a proper if unaccustomed richness was achieved in architecture that proves how valid the craftsman's traditions remained. It would be hard to conjure up grander interiors than those. Enormous spaces (*plate* 73) for the kneeling barons in their ranks were floored with the intricate texture of polished tight-woven straw mats. The Shogun sat on a low dais against gold screens on which Eitoku himself had splashed his ink-strokes. The pillars and rafters were a miracle of delicate simplicity, but studded with chiseled gold-bronze. The ceiling coffers were painted or carved wood panels and, on the moveable side walls enormous formal lions in color tumbled and played. If those walls were slid aside, the gardens of ancient pines and mossy stones, newly laid out by Rikyu the master, led the eye past running water and over still ponds to distant suggestions of ordered park and hillside.

The test of architectural carvings is to examine them, as I have had the luck to do, apart from the structure they adorned. Only technique is then our admiration. Restored again to lintel or squinch or running beam-top, we see them properly an integral part of the palace conception—sheer exuberance of master-craftsmen.

Okakura Kakuzo, in despair at nineteenth century attempts to fuse Japanese style with western requirements, used to say that the Momoyama architects could have accomplished even that. The lost cathedral of Nambanji, built for the use of Christians in Kyoto, was perhaps the perfect solution, for it had been erected by these greatest builders and in the grand manner.

[47]

Thus it will be seen that if architectural carvings of the end of the sixteenth and the early seventeenth century fail to move us as the holy images of Nara and Kamakura do, it is largely because their purpose is not a moving one. The craftsman's aim was perhaps not very high, nor was it single, but he succeeded to the Shogun's taste in carving palace embellishments.

Tokugawa Period

A.D. 1615 TO 1867

DECORATION HIDES FUNCTION.   The later palaces and tombs of Nikko that so take the tourists' breath were made after the death of the first Tokugawa Shogun. One who has felt the severe nobility of ancient and mediaeval Japanese sculpture turns from them with a sense of loss. In Nikko he finds the true spirit of ancient Japan better in the enormous cryptomeria trees that half hide such tortured ornament. In fact this period in aristocratic sculpture under the Tokugawas is, in a sense, the least Japanese of them all. But enough can be seen in *plates* 74 *to* 76 to show that, if the baroque manner of it does not please our modern western taste, the execution was quite as skilled as ever.

CARVING DESERTS BUDDHISM.   But to lament the past glories is but to show that we are following too rigidly one technique and one purpose, and that we have come to its natural end. The shifting truth now lies in the happy fact that revolution had fetched to the surface new patrons with new purposes and a demand for other techniques in sculpture. If much that we had learnt to admire seems now to have been forsaken, it must be noticed that there remains a tradition of noble craftsmanship applied to fresh purpose.

IRON SWORD-GUARDS.   In 1638, with the definite ban on all foreign intercourse, and temporal power now moved from Kyoto to Edo—(the modern Tokyo) we can watch the rise of plebeian

[49]

patronage as well as the pathetic struggles of the older classes to hold their grip on art. In these piping times of peace the gentry of the two courts continued to wear swords and to pay the inlayers and the metal-chiselers to embellish the fittings with the only jewelry that fashion permitted gentlefolk to wear. At first the iron sword-guards had been serviceable enough, and the decoration was mainly sawn out in prim patterns to lighten the weight for the hand, or hammered on the soft iron with admirable restraint. But the Kano school of painting found, in the court armorers, pupils who were all too willing to ape their fashions in a technique entirely alien to that of the smith. Alloys of various colors could now be so cunningly inlaid that one would think them pigments laid on with a flexible brush. For a moment of time both execution and design were masterly. But two generations had barely passed when chiselled surfaces of honest iron were wrought to take on the look of pine bark or a bit of rotten stump. Sheer wearisome dexterity became the fashion. One is, at the last forced to turn away from the armorers and look in still another place for that elusive spark that dodges and dies and glows again through this long brocade that is a nation's history. You will find that spark in a thousand places if you study the textiles, the prints, the lovely lacquers, the domestic architecture and, perhaps best of all, the gardens of Tokugawa times. In sculpture it burns lower and is sometimes almost quenched.

NETSUKE.   Wood and ivory and bone were carved literally into a million shapes for tiny toggles worn by all classes thrust under the sash to hold the strings of pouch or purse or lacquer pill-box. While these *netsuke*, limited in time to three centuries and in space to a size no bigger than your thumb, are not the most important phase of the sculpture of a great nation, they were so considered by certain Europeans in the nineties. At least they were an admirable index of the playful taste of Japan during the last period. They run the whole gamut from the crude and serviceable, through incredible intricacy, to the few master works that show lovely and deliberate simplicity. Another of Okakura's penetrating criticisms—and no-one in our day has given us such penetrating ones about the art of the Far East— was to a pupil who confessed that he was sick of the whole *netsuke*-carving craft, and that if you showed him a great example he would fail, for very boredom, to detect its virtue. "The test is easy. Enlarge it in your mind's eye and set it, huge, in the centre of the Place de la Concorde to let the distracting crowds and taxis circle about it. If it can stand that it is worthy."

One great charm of *netsuke* is the unending variety of folklore and history they illustrate. A lifetime of rather misplaced delight could be employed in research in their infinite topics and in relishing the single attitude or dramatic moment chosen by the carver-illustrator to suggest a story. There are lyrics and poems and historical romances and good bawdy wit in the small compass of these bits of carving. Though they are often signed and the generations of the artists are carefully recorded in books, that ground is too sterile for us to plough again. The least skillful are quite as likely as the most accomplished to fit comfortably in the hand, to hold up the wallet and furnish a moment's pleasure.

[51]

DOLLS AND PUPPETS.   The makers of dolls and of puppets have driven a flourishing trade in the last three centuries and even before. But those earlier than the Tokugawa period had worked in a time when the doll festival had not yet become almost a ritual in all classes. Neither in those days had the enormously popular theatre begun to encourage its much-beloved little sister, the puppet show. An interesting technique was developed in making both doll and puppet-heads, though it does not appear that the same craftsmen catered to both trades. The block-head was carved, preferably of cypress or paulonia wood, and covered with a layer of paste comparable with western gesso. This varies in its composition and the recipes to make it were jealously preserved by guilds and in the families of craftsmen. China-clay and glue are its main ingredients but they were tempered with other substances such as ground shell or rice-paste. The surface, when it is applied in layers and burnished, is a glossy white extremely well suited to receive color. The dolls and puppets were dressed, sometimes sumptuously, and frequently jointed. Certain puppets, notably those used in the drama peculiar to Osaka, were not simple block-heads like the dolls, but carefully contrived hollow skulls containing the running-gear by which the features were moved. The head illustrated on *plate* 85 was made in 1935 by the oldest surviving master of that craft now doomed by the movies. It is provided with no less than six strings: one to open the mouth, one for each sidewise motion of the eyes, one to shut them, one to lift the eye-brows and one to bow the head. Two men are required to keep such a puppet in action. As for the

[52]

carver's art, in this modern example it displays, according to convention, an exquisitely calculated balance of expression—or lack of it—which, when the features are in play, becomes infused with any one of half a dozen emotions demanded by the text that is being recited by the dramatic reader.

Many towns, even quarters of the capital, had their special types of dolls or figures to be obtained nowhere else. Thus Nara has its *Nara ningyo* of bare wood carved with abrupt formal knife strokes, Miyajima its rustic figures made from knotted tree-boles or odd-shaped branches to which a touch of art is given to lend versimilitude; and Kyoto has its smooth gesso-covered heads, vacuous as the classical beauties in the *Tale of Genji*.

PEASANT CARVINGS.   *Plates* 81 *to* 84 have been reserved for a section of Japanese sculpture not recognized by the academies but, as a group, perhaps as well worth our notice as any but the great masterpieces. These have been carved by the honorable unrenowned but are not to be confused with the work of the professionals who produce the dolls and puppets just mentioned. It is in their transparent honesty and the quick response of medium and tools to a living interest that their value lies. But the time has come when even such things are set up in parlors by a generation sick of an empty perfection. For objects once so common as to be quite unregarded they are today strangely hard to find.

MOKUJIKI SHONIN.   Only the last of my group has a serious religious purpose and, though it comes under the head of peasant art, the carver's name is in this case known—Mokujiki Shonin—Friar Raw Vegetables. It would surprise him to know that his works have been reproduced by one of his countrymen in splendid collotype and a sumptuous tome printed on hand-laid paper a full two centuries after they were carved. For he walked the highways and the lanes preaching his kindly doctrine to poor farmers and eating only raw carrots and green stuff. In the villages where he settled for longer or shorter stays his engaging habit was to carve out holy images of a simple sort. And these have been piously traced and recorded in Mr. Yanagi's beautiful book together with some account of his character and of the wonderful cures he made. I have chosen for illustration, one that shows his knife-stroke (*plate* 83). There is little to say of the image except that its style is natural and pious, and not of the academy, and the carving is perfectly sure. It is to be imagined that a true believer finds it as adequate for a symbol as Unkei's best.

For the others that I show, no such serious purpose can be discovered. The god Ebisu with his fishing rod (*plate* 77) sat no doubt under his rustic shelter by a village cross-roads. He is one of the Seven Gods of Good Luck and as such received the friendly respectful homage of passers by. At certain feast days he had his rice and, more frequently, green leaves in a broken pot or a flower from the hedge. To neglect him entirely was possibly no great matter and yet, one wonders.

I am put to it to name a purpose for the others illustrated. They were fun to fashion and were good enough when they were finished to keep in the cottage. Somehow they have survived, a few from the great population of such figures that must have been carved through the centuries. They have no style in common except the style of perfect simplicity and of adequate knowledge of the wood they are made from. They have neither dates nor names to label them and even their purpose is often indefinite. But to comprehend precisely all that is implicit here would be to know the very heart of the Japanese peasantry and that, it must be realized, was the class from which our craftsmen came all through the ages. It is fitting to close this book with a group of their unprofessional carvings of which they were the artists and the patrons as well.

Fogg Museum, Harvard College
        June, 1936

PLATE 1

The history of this figure is lost in antiquity. But since the beginning it has been associated with the ancient monastery, where it stands today, and with the name of Prince Shotoku, who was one of the most earnest and saintly patrons of Buddhism in Japan. Except for detail the figure is cut from a single log and conceived less in the round than as two shallow reliefs, one in front and one behind, meeting at the sides. The halo is of carved wood and the pierced crown is of metal.

KWANNON OF THE YUMEDONO HALL
Suiko Period, 7th Century
WOOD
Horyuji Temple, Nara

PLATE 2

Detail of plate 1

PLATE 3

In the days when Buddhism in Japan was still a foreign religion, practiced only by a few intellectuals, this statue was made by Korean carvers. The Imperial Prince Shotoku set it up in his household chapel, now a nunnery, where it is still revered.

It is constructed from a single tree-trunk. The color and gold were long ago worn from the surface of the hard wood leaving it a lustrous black like ancient bronze. The gracious, rounded surfaces show nothing of the flat knife strokes that were the pride of later Japanese carvers.

KWANNON

Suiko Period, 7th Century

WOOD

Chuguji Temple, Nara

PLATE 4

Detail of plate 3

PLATE 5

This figure can be hardly a generation removed from the similar one shown on *plates 3 and* 4. Like that, it is associated with the name of Shotoku, Prince Regent, who did much to have Buddhism accepted in Japan. Likewise, also, it is made of a single tree-trunk, though in this case barely five feet high and carved from the cypress that is common in Japan. For generations it has been familiarly called "The Kwannon of the Sacred Crown;" but scholars today believe that it represents Maitreya waiting for the enlightenment of the world before he shall accept his full beatitude.

MIROKU
Suiko Period, 7th Century
WOOD
Koryuji, Kyoto

PLATE 6

In the twilight of the Golden Hall of Horyuji Temple (built in A.D. 625) this attenuated wooden image remains, never sharply visible nor clearly to be understood. Even its name is not sure, for it may represent Kwannon or Kokuzo. It may have been carved by the Koreans, brought over to the workshops outside Horyuji, or, less probably, fetched from overseas by them. It is associated with the Imperial family and with their earliest patronage of Buddhism.

KWANNON (OR KOKUZO)
Suiko Period, 7th Century
WOOD
Kondo, Horyuji Temple, Nara

PLATE 7

Detail of plate 6

For the purposes of this book violence has been done to one of the most beautiful and precious of the early wooden images in Japan. The illustration shows only the legs, feet, pedestal, and the thick planks sawn into a formal curving scarf that falls on each side. It demonstrates the comparatively shallow cutting of detail, more like low-relief carving around a cylinder than sculpture conceived in the round.

PLATE 8

In A.D. 625 this bronze triad and its lotus-petal background were made by Tori, the bronze-caster, at the Imperial command. It commemorated Prince Shotoku, Regent of the Empire, who worshipped in this building, and the image still keeps its place. This hall is the oldest wooden structure now in use, and the bronze group shows how close the craftsman—third generation from a Korean, naturalized in Japan—held to a still earlier tradition of Chinese stone-cutters. But the austerity of rock is already tempered by a convention of curves and surfaces appropriate to bronze.

SEATED BUDDHA, WITH ERECT ATTENDANTS, HALF LIFE-SIZE

SUIKO, A.D. 625

By Tori Busshi

BRONZE

Horyuji, Nara

PLATE 9

The sculptured fittings for the Golden Hall at Horyuji Temple seem to have been made by the members of a workshop under the direction of a single master. The angel shown on the left is one of a heavenly choir perched about a wooden canopy suspended over the central dais.

On the right is shown a life-size figure of one of the guardian kings that stand at the four points of the compass. This one, Bishamon Ten, holds a spear and the stupa which is the symbol of the Buddhist church. He tramples on a grotesque spirit, emblem of the evil forces from which he protects the shrine.

A   ANGEL
Suiko Period, 7th Century
WOOD
Kondo, Horyuji Temple, Nara

B   GUARDIAN KING, BISHAMON TEN
Suiko Period, 7th Century
WOOD
Kondo, Horyuji Temple, Nara

PLATE 10

All the larger early Buddhist bronzes of China were long ago melted down for coin or to satisfy the periodic outbursts of anti-Buddhist feeling. None is left. The few that remain in Japan are, therefore, doubly precious and among them are the four statues at Yakushi-ji of which the figure of Gakko is one.

No doubt Chinese or Korean craftsmen worked on this figure and its companions, for they are distinguished by a sure technical perfection that implies previous centuries of practice and of achievement. The style in China had already passed from the severe formality that had marked bronze modelling through the sixth century. With Indian help, the emphasis now shifted toward naturalism and a deliberate loveliness which later proved its undoing. But here is no loss of spiritual quality. The Westerner, to whom the form is strange and the symbol unrecognizable, will find here the very satisfaction he knows in the perfection of the High Renaissance bronzes or Classical ones. In addition, he may find a deeper significance than is usual in those periods in the west.

GAKKO BOSATSU
Hakuho Period, late 7th Century
BRONZE, H. 11 FT. 3 IN.
Yakushiji Temple, Nara

PLATE 11

Detail of plate 10

PLATE 12

Head of colossal seated figure of the god of healing—Yakushi. It is seated as the central figure of the bronze triad of which the left-hand attendant appears on *plates* 10 *and* 11.

The three figures compose the largest group and perhaps the most exquisitely cast bronze sculpture that remains from antiquity in the Far East.

YAKUSHI

DETAIL OF HEAD

Hakuho Period, late 7th Century

BRONZE

Yakushiji Temple, Nara

PLATE 13

This trinity of the god Amida and two attendants is among the most perfect and lovely bronze castings known today. It was not for public worship but for the private chapel of a lady of the Imperial household during the seventh century.

It represents the god in his paradise seated on his lotus which rises from the sacred lake. At the back, in low relief of the utmost delicacy, are heavenly beings also on lotuses. Though probably of Chinese or Korean workmanship, there is reason to believe this group begins to show some elements of the Japanese native style that developed during the next century.

TACHIBANA SHRINE, AMIDA TRINITY
Hakuho Period, late 7th Century
BRONZE
Horyuji Temple, Nara

PLATE 14

Bronze background of the Amida triad shown on *plate* 13. Contrasting with the figures of the three deities before them, the heavenly beings of paradise are rendered in low relief bronze casting. They too are enthroned on symbolic lotuses and their scarfs are blown upward to form a composition of almost unparalleled grace. The pierced bronze lotus halo for the Amida's head is separate and hangs before this screen partly obliterating it.

TACHIBANA SHRINE, AMIDA TRINITY
DETAIL OF BACKGROUND SCREEN
Hakuho Period, late 7th Century
BRONZE
Horyuji Temple, Nara

PLATE 15

The bronze lake surface, from which the lotus pedestals (*plate* 13) emerge, is a formal pattern in low relief. Lily pads and conventional ripples are on its surface. It should be examined in connection with the bronze screen (*plate* 14) set behind it, where heavenly beings in paradise are modelled, and with the triad (*plate* 13), in the full round, sitting on the lotus thrones that grow out of this water.

TACHIBANA SHRINE, AMIDA TRINITY
DETAIL OF LAKE OF PARADISE
Hakuho Period, late 7th Century
BRONZE
Horyuji Temple, Nara

PLATE 16

This plate shows how a five-foot wooden armature was constructed for a hollow lacquer figure. Hemp cloths, treated with lacquer juice, were arranged over this frame and allowed to harden into permanent shape.

The head was made separately, also of layers of lacquered cloth (see *plate* 23) moulded on a clay form and the clay dug out when the lacquer became rigid.

Details were added in a paste composed of lacquer-juice, clay and sawdust. Finally gold leaf and color were added to the surface.

The result was a life-size statue, hollow, light, tough and insect-proof.

ARMATURE FOR HOLLOW LACQUER FIGURE
Nara Period, 8th Century
WOOD
Akishino Temple, Nara

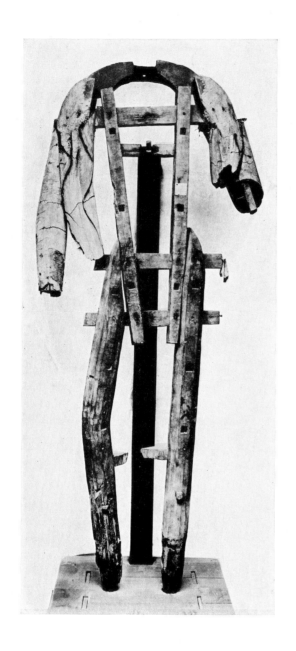

PLATE 17

A pair of menacing guardians stand on opposite sides of the central image of Kwannon in the eighth-century temple of Todaiji. This is one of the pair.

Hollow lacquer, supported internally by a wooden armature, imposed on sculpture a vertical balance and a certain rigidity of posture. The artist was driven by these limitations to concentrate his emphasis on facial expression.

GUARDIAN KING
Nara Period, 8th Century
LACQUER
Todaiji Temple, Nara

PLATE 18

Detail of head of the mate to the figure on plate 17

GUARDIAN KING
Nara Period, 8th Century
LACQUER
Todaiji Temple, Nara

PLATE 19

The statues of ten disciples of the Buddha in Kofukuji are delicate figures in hollow lacquer, somewhat less than life-size. The head of one of these statues is illustrated to show how sensitively expressive this medium could be. The high gods were conceived with far less human expression in this same medium.

KASENYEN, ONE OF THE TEN GREAT DISCIPLES OF BUDDHA
Nara Period, 8th Century
LACQUER
Kofukuji Temple, Nara

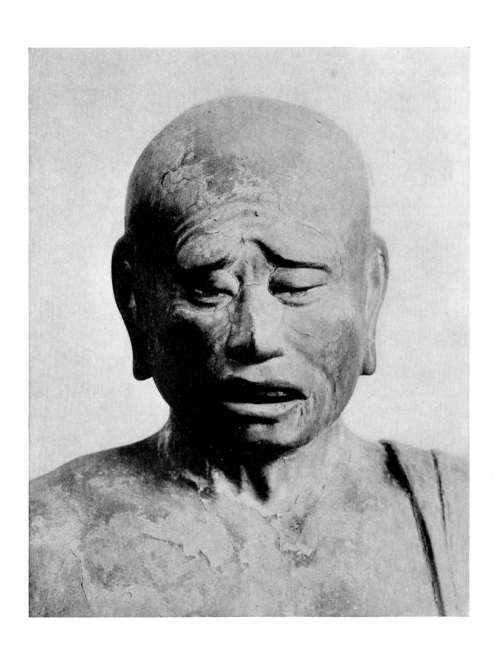

PLATE 20

The eight attendant kings of Buddha are always shown as lesser demi-gods rather than as abstractions. In this example, selected from a series of figures made in hollow dried lacquer, the six arms are symbolic of super-human power. It will be noticed, in contrast, that the face and body are vividly human.

ASHIRA-O

Nara Period, 8th Century

LACQUER

Kofukuji Temple, Nara

PLATE 21

This figure, made by the technique of hemp cloths lacquered together, is the largest left us and is still in excellent condition. It stands, today, in its original temple. Its size can be judged by the fact that on the jewelled crown is set a figure of the god Amida nine inches high in solid silver. The third eye of omniscience is set vertically in the forehead, and a huge black pearl is below it.

FUKUKENJAKU KWANNON
Nara Period, 8th Century
LACQUER
Todaiji Temple, Nara

PLATE 22

This statue, of which the accompanying illustration is a detail, is one of the largest examples remaining in lacquer. The head and shoulders have been selected to show the contrast of the surfaces produced by the carver compared with those made by the modeller.

Precise and schematic as the features are, and as remote from nature, they possess extraordinary non-human beauty.

MINE-NO-YAKUSHI
Nara Period, 8th Century
LACQUER
Horyuji Temple, Nara

PLATE 23

The layers of lacquered hemp cloth, moulded while still flexible to shape this head, can be seen at the neck.

They were shaped about a clay core which supported them till they stiffened; the clay was then dug out, leaving the head hollow. Details were added in a paste made of lacquer mixed with sawdust and clay.

GUARDIAN KING, TAISHAKU TEN
Nara Period, 8th Century
LACQUER
Akishino Temple, Nara

PLATE 24

Particular veneration is attached to this figure, and its shrine is opened only when there is grave national danger or general rejoicing. It is unique among the early examples of unbaked clay in preserving much of the free drapery which, in this example, is supported by copper wire.

GUARDIAN, SHUKONGOJIN
Nara Period, 8th Century
UNBAKED CLAY
Todaiji Temple, Nara

PLATE 25

This statue, with its companion, standing on the high altar at Todaiji and surrounded by other eighth-century sculpture, is as immediately appealing as anything of that time. All its original coloring is lost, and even the significance of the god Bon Ten in that place is now doubtful, but there remains such modelling in clay as one does not find again in the East.

BON TEN
Nara Period, 8th Century
UNBAKED CLAY
Todaiji Temple, Nara

PLATE 26

In the lower story of the seventh-century pagoda of Horyuji monastery are set four separate groups of clay figurines. Arranged like actors in a pantomime, they represent four scenes: the death of Buddha, the worship of the Sacred Relics, Miroku's Paradise, and the Discourse of Yuima with Monju, God of Wisdom.

This figure of Monju, chosen from the last group, though less than three feet high on its pedestal, has in it something of the majesty of the heroic bronzes of the period.

MONJU

Nara Period

UNBAKED CLAY

Horyuji Temple, Nara

PLATE 27

At the risk of sacrificing all Buddhist significance, this detail has been reproduced as the most obvious way to emphasize the bronze-caster's modelling.

Few examples in this medium, East or West, equal it. Possibly none surpasses it.

BUDDHA

DETAIL OF DRAPERY

Nara Period, 8th Century

BRONZE

Kanimanji Temple, Nara

PLATE 28

Detail of plate 27

PLATE 29

This eighth-century bronze gong and stand was imported from China to be used at Todaiji Monastery in connection with the consecration of the great bronze image of Buddha in A.D. 752, or perhaps cast on the spot under the direction of continental craftsmen. No example of greater technical excellence remains in China even among the bronze mirrors. One mirror of this century, with a pattern of dragons closely resembling these, is still preserved in Japan.

From the lion's back an octagonal bronze post is erected. The hind legs and scaly tails of two dragons cling to it while their bodies strain apart to come together in a close hug above. A flat bronze gong hangs from their necks and holds them closer by its weight. Above, their necks wave free, avoiding each other, and the free claw of one upholds the plate where once was balanced the symbol of the Flaming Jewel. Modern bronze-casters have never improved on the technical perfection of this most elaborate work of the Nara Period.

GONG

Nara Period, 8th Century

BRONZE

Kofukuji Temple, Nara

PLATE 30

The bronze Buddha at Nara, now destroyed, was fifty-three feet high. In the spring of 752 it was dedicated in the presence of the Emperor, the court, thousands of clergy, and scores of Chinese and Korean dignitaries.

On the Lotus Throne, several petals of which are still preserved, were engraved symbols of the Thousand Worlds, each presided over by an incarnate Buddha and each containing a hundred million lesser worlds among which our world is but one. This rigid hierarchy of Heavens, presided over by the colossal Buddha of the Law, was seized on by statesmen of the day as sound doctrine to be instilled into the people. The parallel with the Imperial position was obvious.

The detail here selected is part of a group of heavenly beings that surrounds one of the lesser incarnate Buddhas. They are the very draughtsmanship of contemporary China, indelibly graved in Japanese bronze. No more beautiful or characteristic examples have come down to us even in China. Though dating from the period of Japanese apprenticeship, this monument shows the Japanese heritage, their model, and their inspiration.

Engraving on Lotus Petal of the Pedestal of the Daibutsu
Nara Period, 8th Century (A.D. 751)
BRONZE
Todaiji Temple, Nara

PLATE 31

In the middle of the eighth century Chinese and Korean bronze-casters had been invited from the Continent to work on the fifty-three foot statue of Buddha and its bronze liturgical paraphernalia. Among the latter was this great lantern which was set up in front of the temple doors.

On the bronze grilles of the lantern are lions in strange perspective and divine minstrels playing on the flute, flageolet, and cymbals, before the throne of the Buddha of the Law of the Myriad Worlds. The style and technique of this bronze are recognizably those of contemporary China, but no lantern remotely comparable to it remains on the Continent.

LANTERN
Nara Period, 8th Century
BRONZE
Todaiji Temple, Nara

PLATE 32

Detail of plate 31

PLATE 33

This figure was hewn from a single tree-trunk, except for the arms, joined at the elbows, and drapery that was added to hang free from shoulders to base.

Simple chisels and gouges and knives were the tools. Thus the cylindrical trunk was modified by only shallow channels that sweep largely with the grain.

The face, to which the westerner looks for expressive beauty, is properly empty of humanity. It conforms, like the rest of the figure, to the consistent laws of steel on wood rather than to the shapes of flesh and of drapery.

SHUHO-O BOSATSU
Nara Period, 8th Century
WOOD
Toshodaiji Temple, Nara

PLATE 34

This is one of the few early examples of the images made for the practices of the new secret Buddhist sects. By the last decades of the eighth century, when it was made, a great tradition of wood-carving was nearly dead and no new one had been developed. Happily this example is in the old grand manner. The head is nobly blocked out and set above an ample chest. The formal visage is carved in the manner of fifty years before.

YORYU KWANNON
Nara Period, 8th Century
WOOD
Daianji Temple, Nara

PLATE 35

The *Bugaku* Dramas of the eighth century are lost,—text, manner of presentation and purpose. A few strains of music, that are traditionally said to have been used with *Bugaku*, and more than a score of masks, survive. False heads, rather than masks, were worn by actors who postured on open platforms in the temple yard. They were made to be seen in the open and from a distance, in full daylight or by torchlight. Their scale is large and their emphasis on the grotesque. To be comprehended they should be contrasted to rather than compared with the little masks used indoors for the *No* drama of the sixteenth to nineteenth centuries.

DRAMATIC MASK
Nara Period, 8th Century
WOOD
Todaiji Temple, Nara

PLATE 36

From this wooden figure of the seated Buddha, all gold and color have disappeared. There is here a better opportunity to appreciate the formal technique of the wood-carver. (See detail in next plate).

BUDDHA

Jogan Period, 9th Century

WOOD

Muroji Temple, Nara

PLATE 37

Detail of plate 36

This illustration shows the manner in which the long curves and edges were determined by a knife held slantingly upright. The rolling surfaces, across the grain, were completed by chisel and gouge at right angles to the knife-cuts.

This shallow cutting is usually said to have been determined by the designer's brush and has been called "calligraphic." But this detail proves that the curves are those of a knife drawn first with and then gradually across the grain in a single motion.

PLATE 38

We do not know even the name of the Buddhist deity here represented. But, shorn of almost every recognizable feature—hands, feet, color, head—one can the more easily grasp certain naked essentials of wood-carving.

The change of a tree-trunk into a recognizable symbol, and even the knife and chisel-strokes by which this was accomplished, can be better detected in this wrecked image than in any other example illustrated.

The fact that it is headless dispels the western fallacy that facial expression is our main clue to beauty, for this is undeniably one of the most beautiful of Japanese wood-figures. Human shape is here almost absent and we again discover that wood shapes, ably carved, have their beauty independent of humanity.

UNKNOWN NYORAI
Jogan Period, 9th Century
WOOD
Toshodaiji Temple, Nara

PLATE 39

Architectural embellishment of this sort was uncommon at the time (A.D. 1053) when these ornaments were designed for the family chapel of the Fujiwaras. Their scale was so delicate, in comparison with the simple beams, that their value, seen from below, was approximately that of the wall-paintings in the same room. After this period, Buddhist architects made increasing use of carved detail till, by the eighteenth century, the function of building units was obliterated by it.

ARCHITECTURAL CARVINGS

Fujiwara Period, A.D. 1053

WOOD

Ho-o-do, Byodo-in Temple, Uji

PLATE 40

The essence of Fujiwara delicacy is seldom better exemplified than in this diminutive Buddhist angel. Carved from a single piece of wood, even to the flowing scarfs and clouds, it is one of fifty or more similar figures which embellish the halo of Amida, the central deity of the Phoenix Hall in the Byodo-in Temple near Kyoto. Even in so minor a detail as the enrichment of a halo, Jocho, to whom the Amida is attributed, displayed his ingenuity, for no two of the apsaras are precisely alike. Dancers, musicians, votive figures, are all clearly cut—each in its individual pose. Much of their brilliance is now lost; but, originally, against a gold background encircling the great figure of Amida, they must have encouraged many an impatient soul awaiting the bliss of the Western Paradise.

APSARA, ATTRIBUTED TO JOCHO

Fujiwara Period, middle 11th Century

WOOD

Ho-o-do, Byodo-in Temple, Uji

PLATE 41

The thirteenth century image-maker no longer used solid tree-trunks for his statuary. He divided them in better contrived units for his joinery. This badly injured figure shows something of the way the statue looked when it was roughed out and assembled, before it was finished in detail with the addition of lacquer, color and gold.

AMIDA NYORAI
Late Fujiwara or Early Kamakura Period, 12th to 13th Century
WOOD
Fukkiji Temple, Oita Province

PLATE 42

Of special importance to historians of art, this image should be seen complete within its original shrine. Since it is the earliest carved example of a subject not uncommon in painting, it is the more significant to discern how the painter's point of view has influenced the sculptor. The back is flat to allow the figure to be set close to its carved and colored background; the flesh—of which an unusual amount is visible—is colored in ivory white; and the draped-up skirt suggests a design from the brush of a draughtsman rather than by the chisel-user. Westerners may find this image almost bafflingly formal; but the Japanese find it so unconventionally human that its familiar name is the "Fleshly" or "Human-bodied" god.

ICHIJI-KONRIN
Fujiwara Period, middle of the 12th Century
WOOD, PAINTED
Chusonji Temple, Iwate Prefecture

PLATE 43

Kichijoten, goddess of Good Fortune, is traditionally represented as a beautiful lady, richly dressed and adorned with jewels. She stands on a lotus throne and holds in her left hand a pomegranate (or a wishing gem), symbolic of her power to bestow happiness on all who invoke her. This figure, of painted wood, was made during the twelfth century (late Fujiwara); but its full modelling is reminiscent of two or three centuries earlier, when Kichijoten was one of the most popular divinities of Japan. It is remarkable as the only example left us where the painting can be seen in something like its original condition.

KICHIJOTEN
Fujiwara Period, late, 12th Century
WOOD, PAINTED
Joruriji Temple, Kyoto

PLATE 44

Life-size wooden statue of Bishamon, the Guardian King of the North, with two attendants. This group was set up in the tenth century on Mt. Hiye, to replace a similar one made when the capital was established at Kyoto, below the mountain. Among the thousands of statues of this King, this one alone shades his eyes and looks to the distance. He held under his protection the capital city and the Imperial Residence, and guarded them from the evil influences that come, particularly, from the north.

BISHAMON AND ATTENDANTS
Fujiwara Period, 9th to 12th Century
WOOD
Kuramadera Temple, Kyoto Province

PLATE 45

Interior of a small wooden shrine which, when closed, forms an oval pillow. These were used by priests in the days when they travelled Japan, spreading the newly developed doctrines of Paradise. It is made from a hard, close-grained, foreign wood. Monju, the god of Wisdom, is carved seated on his lion, while on the inside of each door two disciples are standing on rocky cliffs. Cut out from one piece of wood, with none of the figures inset, it is a most skilful example of technique. In spite of a scale calculated for minute examination, nothing of grandeur is lost. The nut-brown color of the hard wood is relieved only by the intricate play of its own shadows on its own surface and by the web of cut gold leaf on the background.

MONJU SHRINE

Fujiwara Period, 9th to 12th Century

WOOD

Hojo-in Temple, Koyasan

PLATE 46

The best preserved temple remaining from the aristocratic Fujiwara Period is that of Chusonji, in a northern province remote from Kyoto. An exiled noble brought craftsmen from the capital and set up there a monastery of exquisite buildings provided with elaborate decorations.

Of more than forty temples and houses for three hundred priests, only two remain. One is the builder's mausoleum, lined with smooth, black lacquer, from which, long ago, the original gold leaf was stripped. On the lacquered pillars, banners hung from gilt ornaments of cast bronze that were chased and engraved. Photographs of three of these ornaments are reproduced here.

DECORATIVE HANGINGS AND BANNER TOPS
Fujiwara Period, 12th Century
BRONZE
Chusonji Temple, Iwate Prefecture

PLATE 47

Severe forms, typical of the Kamakura spirit, are illustrated in these Buddhist liturgical objects. The reliquary is built of five geometric units representing, from top to bottom, the elements, ether, air, fire, water, earth.

On its four sides, the square incense burner is engraved with the Guardian Kings of the Cardinal Points.

INCENSE BURNER AND RELIQUARY
Kamakura Period, 13th Century
BRONZE, GILDED
Jodoji Temple, Onomichi, Hiroshima Prefecture

PLATE 48

Dai Nichi (Great Light), surrounded by four attendant deities, sits within a sacred tower erected in A.D. 1223 by the widow of the great General Yoritomo, founder of the Kamakura Shogunate.

The manner of the wood-carving and the smooth lacquer surface of these statues are that of the effeminate art of the previous century, and only by the flat knees and the use of crystal for the eyes could one attribute them to the first quarter of the thirteenth. So, too, the elaborate carving of the thrones has been carried so far as to seem a rather sterile over-refinement of the delicacy of a former period.

The index finger of the god's left hand, clasped by all five fingers of the right, represents, in mystic symbolism, the Six Elements that, united, produce the sixfold happiness of body, intellect and spirit.

DAI NICHI NYORAI AND ATTENDANTS
Kamakura Period, 13th Century
WOOD
Pagoda, Koyasan

PLATE 49

Koben, third son of Unkei, fell direct heir to his father's workshop and traditions. He made this wooden gnome and its mate, half life-size, for the temple of Kofukuji in Nara, the ancient capital. It is quite within the spirit of his age that they were unconventional and were neither god nor man nor any sprite familiar in the ritual. Looked at as a mere support for the lantern, the human figure could be hardly arranged more stably; for the left knee is locked against the down-thrust and the right foot planted wide to make a solid base. The right arm is outstretched, rigid, for a balance.

TENTOKI (LANTERN BEARER)
Kamakura, dated A.D. 1215
By Koben
WOOD, PAINTED
Kofukuji Temple, Nara

PLATE 50

Few carvings of mediaeval Japan can be as closely dated as this one. Although the signature of Tankei does not prove his personal touch, we can take it for granted that it was made in his workshop and after his manner. Compared with the figures carved by him nearly half a century earlier there is loss of vividness and of the conceptions that made Tankei great.

In *plate 52* a single one of these tiny hands is shown to demonstrate the skill lavished on detail which could hardly have been seen by the casual worshipper.

SENJU KWANNON (THOUSAND ARMED KWANNON)
Kamakura Period, late 13th Century
WOOD
Sanjusangendo Temple, Kyoto

PLATE 51

Detail of plate 50

PLATE 52

This gilt wooden hand, holding the flask of the Water of Life, is one of many. Each hand is perfectly conceived and executed. This picture shows the actual size of one of the hands.

HAND
Kamakura Period, 13th Century
WOOD
Sanjusangendo Temple, Kyoto

PLATE 53

The ancient carving formulas employed by generations of image-makers were at first largely the result of knife and of wood-grain and of the symbol-maker's purpose. But, by the thirteenth century, convention somewhat weakened under the pressure of a new interest in naturalism. This mouth and nose and chin are illustrated apart from the whole in order that the knife-strokes may be examined. The original blocked-out features may be imagined as they looked before their shapes were refined.

KWANNON BY JOKEI (dated 1226)
Kamakura Period, 13th Century
WOOD, PAINTED AND GILDED
Kuramadera Temple, Kyoto

PLATE 54

The staff in Jizo's right hand is topped with metal rings that jangle to warn insects and small animals from being trampled. The rings are six in number to symbolize the Sixfold Path of the Buddha. The left hand holds the magic crystal by which prayer is answered.

During the Kamakura period, when the statue was carved, Jizo was an extremely popular divinity; and this delicate shape was evolved by the carver Kaikei, master of Eikai, who signed the statue. Kaikei's influence was so enduring, his pupils so rigidly trained, and the proportions and joinery of image-making so carefully established by him, that his formula persisted for generations.

JIZO
Kamakura Period, 13th Century
WOOD
Chomyoji Temple, Shiga Province

PLATE 55

The secret practices of Buddhist Sects during the twelfth and fourteenth centuries required frequent use of the various Myo-O, terrific forms of divinities otherwise represented as of beneficent aspect. Of the attributes which this Aizen holds, the bow and arrow dispel forgetfulness, the bell awakens enlightenment, the five-pointed *vajra*, held against the breast, symbolizes a pure heart prepared to be enlightened, and the lotus dispels guilt. The lion's head supports another five-pointed *vajra* in the head-dress.

With the new demand for such complications of symbols, the schools of Unkei and Kaikei developed the new skills necessary to render them in sculpture. This image is in their manner and shows the closer likeness to human form needed to express the fresh and more human subdivisions of the Absolute.

AIZEN MYO-O
Kamakura Period, 13th to 14th Century
WOOD
Koizumi Collection, Tokyo

PLATE 56

Large groups of wooden figures assembled in scenes suggesting action were sometimes set up during the twelfth and thirteenth centuries. Though compositions, such as the one from which this was borrowed, were originated by painters, individual figures were rendered at the crest of the sculptor's skill, and his technique showed new scope. Contemporary Chinese art was available again to the Japanese, after centuries of severed relations. This dragon suggests the shapes of Chinese animals in the Sung Period, but the rider and his poise, and the technique of the carving, are as developed in Japan.

ATTENDANT OF FUDO
Kamakura Period, late 12th Century
WOOD
Kongobuji Temple, Okayama Prefecture

PLATE 57

Cousin and contemporary of Unkei, the great innovator among sculptors, Kaikei followed closely in the family tradition of Kyoto image-makers. This seated Buddha, with the right hand raised to preach, is one of the few statues known to have been made by him. Its technical perfection is as great as that of the more rugged and naturalistic work of Unkei, but the result is more formal. Only close examination of the hand, the carving of the lips, etc., brings out the fact that Kaikei delighted in close naturalism of details that did not destroy the abstract quality of the symbol he made. The halo—though its background is a restoration—still supports twelve of the most spirited little angels in Japanese sculpture. Above them is the stupa that held the sacred relics of the Buddha and became a symbol for the Buddhist canon and the church.

SHAKA NYORAI, BY KAIKEI
Kamakura Period, 12th to 13th Century
WOOD
Empukuji Temple, Otsu Province

PLATE 58

By the beginning of the fifteenth century, Unkei's naturalism and Kaikei's lovely line and surface were imitated by their successors. Koen, two generations later than they, was perhaps more successful than any wood-carver of his time in preserving something of the manner of both sculptors.

ANGEL PLAYING A FLUTE

Kamakura Period, 13th Century

WOOD

Koizumi Collection, Tokyo

PLATE 59

The perfect combination of flesh with spirit, in a single wood figure, was perhaps most nearly achieved by Unkei and his followers. Buddhist sculpture before their time held more of the spirit; after them it lapsed to conventionality or sculptors were diverted to non-religious work. This lank figure, holding a sacred scroll in his hand, would totter if it were not for the staff braced under the elbow. There is an ingenious but convincing system of struts and braces; the weak knees, rickety spine, and holy book, are propped by the staff.

VASUBANDHU, ATTRIBUTED TO TANKEI

Kamakura, middle of 13th Century

WOOD, PAINTED

Rengeoin, Sanjusangendo, Kyoto

PLATE 60

Among the many memorial portrait statues of mediaeval Japan, this is perhaps the only one that is definitely known to have been carved during the lifetime of the original. It is signed and dated twenty years before the Shogunate moved its headquarters from Kamakura back to Kyoto, when the sitter was eighty-four years old. There is obvious reason to believe that it was done from the living model. But graphic and lively though it is, the remarkable fact remains that this face and figure are no whit more convincing than those of the Emperor Go Shirakawa's portrait statue (*plate* 62), done of a person two centuries dead. The conclusion is that Kamakura sculptors, particularly those of the Zen Buddhist School, concentrated their efforts on expressing the character of a sitter as their imaginations pictured it. Thus to catch a likeness of a living or a dead character presented the same problem. Here, as in *plate* 63, the proportions of the body and the hang of drapery are schematically imagined and formally executed. The face (in reality hardly less formal) is cunningly wrought to produce that effect of life which we consider non-formal or individual.

MEMORIAL STATUE OF THE PRIEST KOREKATA OF THE ZEN SECT
Kamakura Period, c. A.D. 1372
WOOD
Hokwaiji Temple, Kanagawa Prefecture

PLATE 61

A portrait of Muso Kokushi (the Abbot Soseki). The body and robes are so formally executed that the attention insensibly comes to rest on the head, here shown. Friend of an Emperor, advisor to the Shogun's court during the turmoil of civil wars, he pursued the arts of peace undisturbed. He so organized the temples and monasteries of his Zen sect that their influence survived for centuries. He saw to it that at least one Zen temple was set up in each province and neither heresy, popular neglect, nor financial difficulties destroyed them. Patron of the arts, his own particular arts were those of literature and the garden. In the latter he was past master.

This statue may well have been made from life or from vivid memory by a carver who knew him.

PORTRAIT OF THE ABBOT SOSEKI

Kamakura Period, 14th Century

WOOD

Zuisenji Temple, Kanagawa Prefecture

PLATE 62

Two full centuries must have elapsed after the death of the Emperor before this extraordinarily vivid portrait-statue was carved. It is, therefore, impossible to consider it a likeness. But portraiture in the most literal sense it is. Lacking the original face to copy, the sculptor copied his mental image of the famous Emperor, and the result is as vivid and convincing as any woodcarving can be. The Emperor reigned but two stormy years during the civil wars between turbulent clans. He abdicated, assumed the Buddhist priesthood and was an ardent believer in Honen's Pure Land doctrines. For the next thirty-four years he controlled his three successors on the throne.

The precise pyramid of brocade, topped by a shaven skull and intellectual enigmatic face, is at the same time naturalistic and an obvious happy device to focus attention on the visage.

EMPEROR GO SHIRAKAWA
Kamakura Period, late 14th Century
WOOD
Chokodo Temple, Kyoto

PLATE 63

Zen Buddhism, through its emphasis on individual character, encouraged the making of human portraits. Sacred as well as lay sculpture in the thirteenth century dwelt on human qualities and expression. This was the easier for the carver because of Unkei's improvements in the technique of wooden image-making and his method of carving a light face or mask that could be worked separately from the rest of the figure. The formal pyramid of court dress and cap shown in this portrait are by no means a mere artist's conventions. This is a precise rendering of the attitude and outlines of a noble seated in his stiff brocades.

MEMORIAL STATUE OF UESUGI SHIGEFUSA
Kamakura Period, 13th Century
WOOD
Meigetsuin Temple, Kanagawa

PLATE 64

The evangelist Kuya is represented crying his formula for salvation in the streets. Kamakura naturalism was never carried further than in this portrait-like figure. It is the more startling therefore to see issuing from his mouth a stiff row of little images of the god Amida whose name he invokes and whose mercy he explains to the people. He carries a staff tipped with staghorn, and a mallet with which to beat the gong that hangs about his neck.

THE PRIEST KUYA, BY KOSHO
Kamakura Period, 13th Century
WOOD
Rokuharamitsuji Temple, Kyoto

PLATE 65

Detail of plate 64

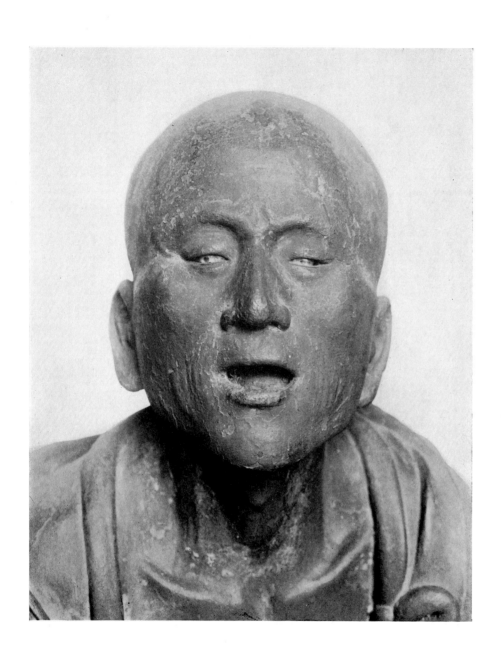

PLATE 66

This gilt bronze reliquary for sacred bones is in the form of a shrine lantern. No more perfect or elegant example is known. An enlarged detail of the grille, in the next illustration, shows how cast bronze has been refined by chisel and graver. The surface has been fire-gilt to make the delicate design still more vivacious.

Since most of our bronze from this period is confined to specimens of sword furniture or to figures of the gods, this reliquary is all the more important as an example of fourteenth-century skill.

RELIQUARY
Kamakura Period, 14th Century
BRONZE, GILDED
Saidaiji Temple, Nara

PLATE 67

Detail of Grille, plate 66

PLATE 68

Ippen Shonin, the itinerant preacher, is shown walking and in the act of invoking the god Amida with the famous formula *Namu Amida Butsu*. It was a common practice before his time; but he was the first to preach the doctrine that Amida's power is so great he brings to his paradise any one—believer or non-believer—who repeats those words.

Carved two centuries after the death of the saint, likeness was impossible. But there is a convincing power in the figure that is an adequate substitute for lifelikeness.

THE PRIEST IPPEN, BY MICHI NAO
Ashikaga Period, dated 1495
WOOD
Hoganji Temple, Iyo Province

PLATE 69

Architectural ornament, still much restrained and little used in the fifteenth century, is well worth study in view of its luxuriant growth in the next three centuries. These two beam-ends, added during repairs to the ancient temple of Horyuji in the Ashikaga period, show how adequate and truly structural such embellishment was. The ends project from the pillar-tops which support them, carry no weight, and are in the open air and sun. Originally they were colored.

CARVED BEAM ENDS

Ashikaga Period, mid 15th Century

WOOD

Horyuji Temple, Nara

PLATE 70

Such light-weight masks as this supplanted the great false heads used out of doors for the earlier religious dramas (see *plate 35*). Examples as early as the one shown here are rare, though later they were produced by the thousand for the amateur actors of miracle plays.

The heavy shadows and rugged emphasis are in the manner of the sculptors of a previous century, but from this time the convention turned toward smooth and shallow planes of more subtlety.

No Drama Mask, by Sankobo

Ashikaga Period, c. 1470

WOOD

Imperial Household Collection, Tokyo

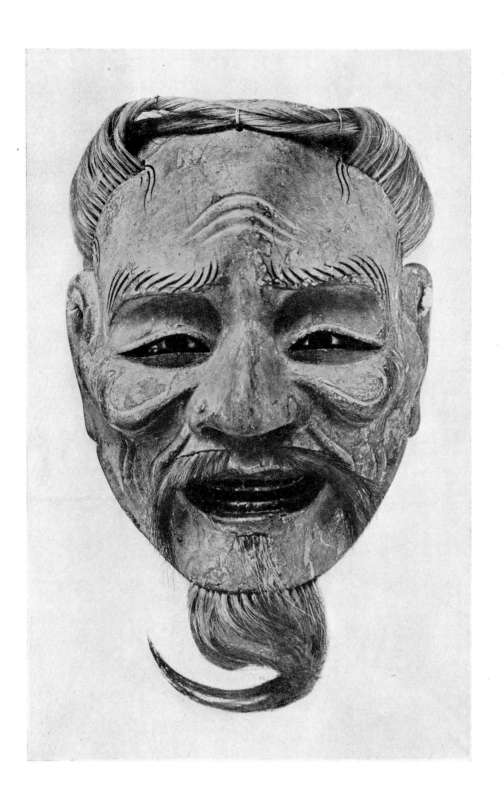

PLATE 71

The palace built at Momoyama, by the parvenu Taiko Hideyoshi (see text), has supplied the name for the period (1568-1615) and the name has become a symbol for elaborate splendor. This was one of the lesser entrances to that palace—happily saved and moved to the temple of Nishi Hongwanji in Kyoto after the Taiko's death. Although the architectural style is called Chinese and undoubtedly owes something of its appearance to the later Mings, the sculpture employed has little Chinese about it except the subjects chosen. This gate and the ample audience chamber moved to the same temple (*plate 73*) are the only important units left us from the architecture in the grand manner of that period. They are doubly precious since they show the very limit to which embellishment was carried before it encroached on the functional shapes, to warp and hide them.

GATE FROM HIDEYOSHI'S PALACE AT MOMOYAMA

Momoyama Period, 16th Century

WOOD

Now at Nishi Hongwanji Temple, Kyoto

PLATE 72

Door. *Detail of plate 71*

PLATE 73

In these great spaces the ranks of barons knelt in audience before the dais of the Shogun. Behind and beside his seat were gold and silver screens painted by Kano Eitoku and by Sanraku. The pillars and beams were chosen for their perfect grain, unhidden by paint. The rafters were socketed with chased, gilt bronze; the spike-heads were gilt and engraved.

The wooden grille, supporting the ceiling, marks the division of the higher nobility from those of lesser rank. On such carvings the most skilful sculptors lavished their work.

CONVOCATION HALL OF NISHI HONGWANJI TEMPLE
Momoyama Period, 16th Century
Nishi Hongwanji Temple, Kyoto

PLATE 74

About the Shogun's tombs, shrines and palaces at Nikko, wood sculpture is employed so lavishly that only its calculated scale can save it from restlessness. In this illustration the freely carved panels are of uniform shape and set in a row rigidly confined between the horizontal lines of the long roof and the stone foundations of the corridor. Over them are set pierced grilles of ripples and floating blossoms, half-hidden in the shadow of the eaves.

The beam-ends of the well-house are elaborate and so, too, are the colored carvings above them, but the stark posts and massive granite basin are more conspicuous than this detail. *Plate 75* shows the manner in which the carvers of these decades contrived to enrich architecture.

CORRIDOR, GATE AND WELL HOUSE
Tokugawa Period, built in 1636
Toshogu Shrine, Nikko

PLATE 75

The shrines at Nikko, where the Tokugawa Shoguns were buried, included palaces for the living as well as tombs for the dead. In rooms of state, such as these, the living Shogun received and even the Imperial Prince held court.

The carved wood panels of the Shogun's phoenix room are polished black-wood enriched with inlay of tortoise-shell, porcelain, horn and lacquer. The lacquered pillars have chased, gilt, bronze fittings, the beams are minutely carved, and between them are brilliantly painted grilles of sculptured wood.

Here, the combination of sculpture, lacquer, and chiselled bronze, is, East or West, unrivalled for splendor.

PHOENIX HALL
Tokugawa Period, 17th Century
Toshogu Shrine, Nikko

PLATE 76

The scores of thousands of holiday-makers coming to the Nikko Shrines each year spend hours admiring the detailed carving of the panels on this gate. Exuberant though this sculpture is, the naturalism is restrained between rigid posts and beams, and minute detail counts merely for pleasant light and shade and color till one steps close.

If the seventeenth and eighteenth-century wood-carvers can be accused of encroaching on the field of painting, it should be remembered that the religious impetus was weak and aristocratic patronage ostentatious rather than wise.

PANELS FROM THE YOMEIMON PALACE GATE
Tokugawa Period
Nikko

PLATE 77

This three-foot wooden image, compared with the subject shown on *plate 82*A, differs entirely in style and manner of carving. The other is but six inches high and might be almost described as low relief on a cube. This one is composed of a series of conventional convex planes with sharp intersections. Perhaps it is more truly conceived in the round.

Ebisu is the only member of the Seven Gods of Good Luck that is purely Japanese in origin. He is almost invariably shown with his *tai* fish and rod. He is frequently venerated independently from the others, and several temples and thousands of road-side shrines are devoted to him.

Although it may be no great sin to neglect him, flowers are still found before his image and, in October, there are offerings of rice.

EBISU

Tokugawa Period, 17th to 18th Century

WOOD

William Rockhill Nelson Gallery of Art, Kansas City, Missouri

PLATE 78

No doubt this foot-high image of some forgotten priest was set up after his death in the chapel where he served. It is, of course, known that, although called a portrait, physical resemblance was not considered. Obviously, such efficient and summary carving was never done by a casual amateur. It is the product of an image-maker of competence.

PRIEST

Tokugawa Period, 17th to 18th Century

WOOD

William Rockhill Nelson Gallery of Art, Kansas City, Missouri

PLATE 79

The foreigner can read little in the benign wrinkled visage concerning the character of the artist Koetsu. But among all those in Japanese history, hardly one was so versatile and cultivated or more charming. The greatest connoisseur of swords that had been known for centuries, he was the unquestioned master of his generation in painting, pottery, calligraphy, carving, landscape gardening and the tea ceremony. A few objects in the various mediums remain from his hand. Thousands of copies and forgeries preserve something of his inimitable point of view.

The figure—a foot and a half high—was carved by Koho, Koetsu's grandson, from the wood of a famous plum tree, called "The Starry Plum." It perhaps contains more of the elements of likeness than was usual in such memorial images.

MEMORIAL IMAGE OF KOETSU, BY HONNAMI KOHO (1601-1682)

Tokugawa Period

WOOD

Koetsuin Shrine

PLATE 80

The Netsuke is a button or toggle tucked under the sash to hold up a pouch or a pill box. They were conceived in innumerable forms. No better field for the study of folklore and popular humor of the last three centuries can be found. Some of the best carvers made *netsuke* to the neglect of Buddhist images and other forms that had in the past claimed undivided attention. The two examples here illustrated are of hard wood. One represents a tree-frog clinging to a pumpkin stem, the other, Shoki the Demon Queller, sharpening his sword.

NETSUKE
Tokugawa Period
WOOD
Museum of Fine Arts, Boston

The Sword Guard of iron is pierced with a wedge-shaped hole for the blade and often has oval holes for the small knives socketed in the scabbard.

Four methods of embellishment are shown here. On the lower left is direct pierced-work made with a saw. It represents geese flying down past the moon, which appears over a cloud-bank. Another shows bamboo leaves in plain piercing further embellished by detail chiselled in slight relief. The decoration of the other two examples is no longer sheer pattern accomplished in one or two processes. They present landscapes pictorially, making a deliberate and successful attempt to use methods developed in painting. The palette is limited to the colors of various alloyed metals inlaid or encrusted. The draughtsmanship is limited by the possibilities of the graving-tool, the chaser and punch.

SWORD GUARDS (TSUBA)
Tokugawa Period
IRON
Museum of Fine Arts, Boston
Collection of Howard Mansfield, Esq., New York

PLATE 81

A

This example of Daikoku is the most formal and conventionalized specimen of the *nata-tsukuri*, sickle-stroke, method of carving which we show. He is recognizable only by the sack of treasure on his back and has barely emerged from the block of wood. But no one should make the mistake of believing that this is an unfinished figure. The symbol is completely recognizable and the maker saw no need for more refinement.

DAIKOKU

Tokugawa Period

WOOD

Yamanaka Collection, Osaka

B

The Minister of State, Tenjin, in his voluminous court brocades, rides to exile on a bull. He was banished by court intrigue in the ninth century and after death his ghost returned to haunt his enemies. As the Thunder God, he set fire to the palace and, as the Pox, he brought disease. Patron of poets and of practicers with the writing brush, he caught the popular imagination.

TENJIN

Tokugawa Period

WOOD

Yamanaka Collection, Osaka

PLATE 82

A

Ebisu is one of the seven gods of good Luck. The red-fleshed *tai* fish (his emblem) is eaten on festival days, particularly at the New Year, because of its auspicious color and its association with the god. (See *plate* 77 for a different rendering of the same subject). This example is a modified variation of the *nata-tsukuri*, sickle-stroke, and is less abrupt than that of the Daikoku on the same page. The flat knife-cuts are rounded, but the wood block still controls the form, and the detail is little deeper than chip-carving. The characteristic hump-back of the fish has been ingeniously and simply made to conform to the surface of the block.

Eʙɪsᴜ

Tokugawa Period

ᴡᴏᴏᴅ

Yamanaka Collection, Osaka

B

Daikoku, one of the seven gods of Luck, appears in a thousand forms. Hardly a household, gentle or simple, was without him. His original significance was long ago transmuted by familiar use, though he is still found at the portals of the temples. In this wooden image he stands on the rice bales of Plenty and holds in one hand the miner's hammer for chipping out ore and jewels in the mine. The other hand holds the neck of his bag filled with treasures. He is the god of commerce who brings riches to tradespeople and the god of good harvest of rice, one grain of which bears manifold. On the sixty-first day of the year the householder offers him one hundred black beans. Being fat, he is a kitchen god.

Dᴀɪᴋᴏᴋᴜ

Tokugawa Period

ᴡᴏᴏᴅ

Yamanaka Collection, Osaka

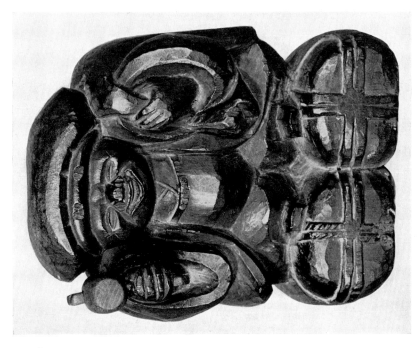

PLATE 83

Mokujiki, the peasant priest who carved this head, wandered from village to village healing and preaching to the farmers. He was not a trained artist but he acquired sufficient skill to make vivid and striking symbols for local worship.

BUDDHIST FIGURE
Tokugawa Period, early 18th Century
WOOD
Photograph, M.Yanagi, Tokyo

PLATE 84

An ancient folk-tale, here illustrated by some village wood-carver, tells of the strong lad, Kintoki, orphaned and found straying by Yama-uba, the Woman of the Mountains. She nursed him and taught him to be companion of the bear and the fox and the rabbit, till Yorimitsu saw his great strength and took him for his squire. The mountain woman is recognized by her traveller's straw hat, with the robust, naked, boy at her feet. Often Kintoki is shown wrestling with his animal friends or pushing down a huge pine to make a bridge for them to cross a torrent. The story is beloved of simple folk and has a hundred varieties. They are popular in the theatre and with the humbler craftsmen who make the toys and the pictures that perpetuate a nation's folklore.

YAMA-UBA AND KINTOKI

Tokugawa Period

WOOD

Yamanaka Collection, Osaka

PLATE 85

A

On the right is a conventional doll of carved wood spread with smooth white gesso for the flesh parts and with full color to represent brocaded garments. It shows Tenjin, the exiled official, patron of poets and calligraphers. Made toward the end of the last century, it is a typical product of the ancient craft of doll-makers in Kyoto.

DOLL
Tokugawa Period
WOOD
Yamanaka Collection, Osaka

PLATE 85

B

On the left is shown the head of a dramatic puppet used in the name-part of the historical melodrama *Matsuo Maru*. It was carved in 1935 by the last remaining master of this art, Tengu-Kyu. The strings, seen at the bottom, are hidden by an elaborate costume. They control no less than seven separate life-like motions: raising and lowering the head, dropping the eyes, turning them to right and to left, raising the eyebrows and opening the mouth. The puppet drama of Osaka city, which has been developed to great perfection, is now being driven out by the cinema.

PUPPET HEAD, BY TENGU-KYU
Modern
WOOD

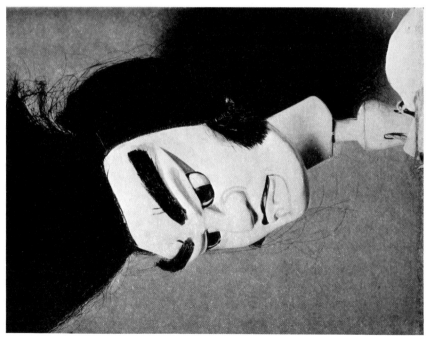

PRINTED AT THE MORRILL PRESS